"Shortchanged *should be read by
every wife who wants to put her marriage
back on the road to success.*"

— H a r v i l l e   H e n d r i x ,   P h . D .

SHORTCHANGED

WHAT YOU GAIN WHEN YOU CHOOSE TO LOVE HIM...OR LEAVE HIM

ELLEN SUE STERN

BANTAM BOOKS
NEW YORK · TORONTO · LONDON · SYDNEY · AUCKLAND

To Zoe and Evan,
for teaching me about love.

Author's Note

*Names and other details of all the people in this book
who talked to me about their lives have been changed
to protect their privacy. I hope that in changing names
I have not unintentionally hit on the names of real-life
individuals who feel the circumstances described could
apply to them. If this has happened, it is purely by
coincidence.*

Library of Congress Cataloging-in-Publication Data
Stern, Ellen Sue, 1954–
  Shortchanged / Ellen Sue Stern.
    p.   cm.
  Includes bibliographical references.
  ISBN 0-553-35291-1 (trade pbk.)
    1.   Marriage—United   States.   2.   Interpersonal
relations.   3. Intimacy (Psychology)   I. Title.
HQ734.S864   1991   *91-3499*
306.81—dc20   *CIP*

*Published simultaneously
in the United States andCanada*

PRINTED IN THE UNITED STATES OF AMERICA
FFG   0   9   8   7   6   5   4   3   2   1

ACKNOWLEDGMENTS

This is the part I look forward to, getting to say thank you to the friends and collaborators who hung out with me during the writing of this book.

First, to Gary. In many ways this book is our final journey. I am forever grateful for your love, your intelligent input, and your willingness to share.

To Jill Edelstein: Your endless patience, humor, and support pulled me through so many tough moments. I love you, my friend.

To Beverly Lewis: My gratitude for your continuing involvement in my work and my life.

To Jonathon and Wendy Lazear: My appreciation for believing in me once again. To the Lazear Agency staff, my thanks for all your support.

To Pamela Espeland: Your thoughtful editing added so much. It's great to work with you!

To Joel Hodroff: I will always be grateful for your boundless enthusiasm and feedback.

To Bonnie Dickel and Steven Kaplan: My heartfelt appreciation for your brainstorming in helping name this book.

*"It is only with the heart that one can see rightly;
what is essential is invisible to the eye."*

— Antoine de Saint-Exupery

The Little Prince

Contents

FOREWORD

A young woman handed me a book entitled *Everything Men Know About Women*. I eagerly opened it; every single page was blank.

I've seen lots of similar jokes as I've traveled across the country over the past couple of years, speaking to women who attend my Expecting Change and Indispensable Woman workshops. Jokes like: "Why did the man cross the road?" "Who knows. Why the hell do they do anything?"

Funny, in a patronizing sort of way. Underneath the sharp edge, though, a central theme has emerged: Many women are *stuck*! Angry at their mates for sins of the past and the present. *Stuck* in a state of chronic disappointment and lowered expectations. *Stuck* in a pattern of sexual withholding, yet desperately in need of warmth and nurturing from their mates.

I've discovered that many women have built a wall of anger and disappointment that blocks their husbands' attempts at warmth and intimacy and prevents the women themselves from appreciating the good in their relationships. Despite their demands for intimacy, they push their husbands away.

Most of the women who have expressed this feeling of chronic disappointment secretly believe that their husbands are to blame for the problems in their marriage, a belief reinforced by the daily onslaught of books and talk shows focused on topics such as why men can't be intimate and how to live with a difficult man. *She* may have a few trivial adjustments to make, but *he's* the one in need of an overhaul. *He's* the "identified patient," whereas *she* expends great sums of energy diagnosing him, issuing her Rx, charting his progress, and waiting for him to get well. Even when *he* shows "improvement," *she* maintains a clinical—and superior—distance: always prepared for a setback, always keeping one foot out the door of the relationship.

I'm not surprised by how many women are discontented, cynical, and bruised. I am, however, surprised by how readily women admit responsibility for patronizing and pushing away their mates. Most important, I am encouraged by how eagerly they welcome the opportunity to heal, to choose whether to love him or leave him, and then to confidently move forward.

Moving forward requires motivation, confidence, and trust that the results will justify the effort. It requires a belief that action equals empowerment—that it is more satisfying to work on strategies for change than to sit around complaining. It requires forgiving the past, making peace with what's possible without compromising our own bottom line, and it requires holding fast to a vision of equal partnership.

This vision is in the spirit of the "second stage" of feminism in which women and men work together to build a new order. Women who are ready to stop being shortchanged are pioneers of the second stage. For this reason it's helpful to look at how this book reflects the evolution of male/female relationships, beginning with Betty Friedan's *The Feminine Mystique,* which exposed women's subservient roles in relation to men and sparked the beginning of the women's movement. This initial awakening—a time of excitement and revolution—led women to express their anger and insist on equality.

Political gains followed—particularly in the workplace—and although the battle is far from won, women *have* grown in position and power. By contrast, however, our love relationships have lagged behind. Many women have fallen into the trap of separatism and superiority out of sheer disappointment. We have settled for seeing men as adversaries, not allies. We assume our mates are limited by virtue of their gender—that they belong to a foreign species and will never be our true equals. We believe this is the best we can hope for, while in fact, it is just a new way of remaining passive and keeping ourselves stuck.

It is again time for women to take control of our lives, this time by fighting for what we want with our mates. In essence there are two choices: to get in or get out.

The first step is to break the pattern and stop focusing on what's wrong with *him*. If we are genuinely interested in improving the quality of our relationships, we need to figure out what *we* want and how *we* can go about getting it. Not because we are the guardians of intimacy, not because it is up to us to do all the work in our relationships, and not because we are transferring the blame back onto ourselves. Responsibility and blame are not synonymous. Rather, we need to approach our relationships in a new way for our own sakes. So that no matter what happens, we know in our hearts that we've gone the distance. That we've given it everything we've got.

The search for how to stop feeling shortchanged by our mates also reflects the basic principles of the recovery movement that is sweeping America. In many ways this is a recovery book; its message is consistent with twelve-step tenets that encourage us to let go of controlling behavior, take responsibility for our actions, and refocus on how we can be our best selves. On the highest level, breaking the pattern of being shortchanged is a spiritual challenge requiring a leap of faith. When individuals approach each other gently and without judgment, they form a sacred partnership, and engage in a process of recovering love.

This book is intended for women searching to make good relationships better, for those in transition, and for those struggling in painful situations. Writing it helped me find greater peace and clarity in my own marriage and in my life. I hope it does the same for you.

One

SHORTCHANGED

The other day I saw a T-shirt that read, "If they can send a man to the moon, why can't they send them all?" At first I laughed out loud. Then I thought about it and decided that banishing men from our lives isn't really the answer. It would be much too easy, for one thing, and in the end we'd be cheating ourselves out of the love we want and deserve.

But for many women, face-to-face with decidedly earthbound men, the prospect of working things out with our mates feels exhausting and overwhelming. It seems unlikely the results will match the effort. We wonder, Why is love so much work? When did they begin to seem like "the enemy" rather than friends, lovers, the ones we most want to share our lives with? When did we get so cynical about love?

"Men just don't get it!" a woman protests to a group of friends. Her comment is greeted by knowing looks and a chorus of "Ahas!" as if their club's secret motto had been spoken. All these women are involved in committed love relationships, yet many adopt a patronizing tone when discussing their mates, cracking jokes about their inferiority and expendability. They disparage them, talk about them as if they were children, or dismiss the possibility of getting more of the love and support they need. Male bashing—the fashionable practice of putting men down for being insensitive or incapable of commitment— is part of a cultural movement. A movement going nowhere.

Men may not *ever* "get it," if "getting it" means responding with the interpersonal finesse that women have been brought up to cultivate and value. Men have never, and may never, give emotionally in the same ways that women do. But as long as we choose men to be our partners to love and to live with, we must stop buying into stereotypes of female superiority and male ineptitude, and instead accept the differences in how men and women relate. As long as we believe that there is a built-in ceiling to what men can give, we limit what's possible between us. When we automatically assume he isn't "educable," that he's genetically incapable of understanding us, and that it's not worth it to go after what we want, then *we shortchange ourselves.* We remain stuck, angry about what we're not getting, but paralyzed to do anything positive about it.

It's no secret that men are responsible for their share of the bad (and the good) in our relationships. But it is not my intention here to focus on men. This book is primarily for and about *women,* about what *we* can do to put everything we've got into making our marriage great or getting out and on with our lives. My aim is to help us see how we put up barriers to intimacy and how to take them down. That way, whether we stay or leave, we'll know we've given it our all.

Instant transformations are unlikely, but improvement is absolutely within our reach *if* we're willing to work on it with our mates. There's good reason to do so, especially as we see more men changing in the ways we've hoped for. Many men *are* coming around, slowly but surely taking on a greater share of parenting and domestic responsibilities, and, in many cases, becoming more emotionally accessible. It's in our own best interest to acknowledge the positive moves men are making, rather than hold on to some fictitious ideal.

A Sign of the Times

An article titled "The New Marital Therapy," published in the *New York Times Magazine* in March 1985, suggested that women, tired of waiting for things to change, were turning off and rejecting genuine efforts on the part of men to forge more intimate bonds. The author wrote, "It is a stunning measure of societal change that most divorces today are initiated by women, and that increasingly treatment is initiated by men, according to therapists across the country."[1]

The article jarred me. What's going on? I thought, my mind reeling with images of men lining up outside therapists' offices and women marching off to divorce courts. Was a revolution stirring? I couldn't shake the feeling that something *was* qualitatively changing between men and women.

In fact, change *is* in the air. The way women relate to men is undergoing a profound shift. So are the expectations we have of our relationships. Many of our fathers sat at the dinner table, never lifting a finger, while our mothers waited on them. If *our* husbands act that way, they're likely to get a wet dishcloth in the face, or at least, be firmly reminded where the kitchen is.

In the same vein, we're less protective of our mates, and more willing to expose their shortcomings. Our mothers and grandmothers experienced discontent and frustration in their marriages, but up until the beginning of the women's movement, those feelings were locked away, expressed only in grumbling or sarcastic comments. "Stand by Your Man" was the national anthem; anything less implied you were less of a woman.

Today that taboo has been broken. Women feel more comfortable, even ennobled discussing their mates' flaws. Particularly in the encounter groups of the sixties and seventies where women formally supported one another in acknowledging and coming to terms with the realities in their relationships, this kind of sharing has been helpful and even life changing.

Indeed, there is a "women's reality," but there is an evolving men's reality too, and it is equally worthy of respect. In her book *The Second Stage,* Betty Friedan states:

I believe that men are at the edge of a momentous change in their very identity as men, going beyond the change catalyzed by the women's movement. It is a deceptively quiet movement, a shifting in direction, a saying "no" to old patterns, a searching for new values, a struggling with basic questions that each man seems to be dealing with alone.[2]

It's time to take steps to heal our differences, with mutual respect and appreciation as the goal. Both women and men face enormous challenges. Women feel pressured to assume multiple roles as workers/mothers/housewives/shoppers/chauffeurs/counselors/social secretaries (the list goes on and on), all of this in the face of inadequate support systems in the workplace and absence of true partnership at home. Men face ongoing pressure to provide financial security, to expand their role in the home, to be simultaneously strong and soft, warrior and creator. And men continue to suffer from the pressure to engage in macho posturing and from lack of support for an honest and expressive emotional life.

We will never have what we want with men until we are willing to acknowledge their humanness, just as we expect them to acknowledge ours. Throughout this book, we will examine ways in which both women and men have been acculturated to be ambivalent about intimacy, and we will explore ways to turn that around. We will concentrate on the part of ourselves that remains hopeful, nurturing our impulses to reach across the gulf and do all we can to have a more satisfying connection with our mates.

What Do Women Really Want?

Most women can easily reel off their list of grievances against their mates. We're much less able to articulate our vision of what would constitute a successful relationship. It's easier to know what's wrong than what would make it right.

What's lacking is intimacy. What do we mean by *intimacy*? Being supported, respected, and understood, for starters. How intimacy is defined and played out in each relationship depends on individual needs and values. For some women, support means concrete help with everyday tasks, whereas other women primarily seek emotional sustenance—a mate who will listen carefully to their feelings and offer thoughtful feedback. Every one of us wants our feelings and needs respected, whether that means more effort on his part to be emotionally and physically close or to honor our need for distance. Being understood— the deep sense that our mates know who we really are on the inside—makes us feel safe, secure, and truly loved.

"I'm searching for my soulmate," "I just wish we could talk more," "I'd be thrilled if he'd spend more time with the kids and help out around the house," women say. Some women crave passionate lovemaking; others simply wish he would put away the groceries. Not every woman is interested in cultivating a deep and intense connection. Despite stereotypes of women wanting to merge body and mind with their lovers, some would rather *not* be that close. One woman fantasizes about growing old peacefully with her husband. Another woman hopes to have the Love Affair of the Century. "A love affair is the last thing on earth I'd want with my husband," counters another. "I just want him to talk to me!"

What women share is the desire to have a better and more fulfilling relationship with their husbands. But we don't know how to start making the changes that would move our relationship in the right direction. We are disappointed because the promises didn't pan out and we don't know what to expect anymore. We are searching for answers to questions such as:

Why am I so angry?

What is the difference between compromise and settling?

Am I holding on to my hurt as a weapon against him?

When does self-protection turn into self-imprisonment?

What is my bottom line?

What are the real reasons I'm with him?

What if he doesn't change no matter how hard I try?

When is it important to keep giving?

When is it time to give up?

Is it possible to start over?

Throughout this book we will explore the answers to these and other challenging questions.

WHY CAN'T A MAN BE MORE LIKE A WOMAN?

When speaking to women's groups, I often quote writer Anna Quindlen's line: "Have you noticed that what passes as a terrific man would only be considered an adequate woman?" She goes on to say,

> What I expect from my male friends is that they are neat and clean. What I expect from my female friends is unqualified love, the ability to finish my sentence for me when I am sobbing, a complete and total willingness to pour out their hearts, and, the ability to tell me why the meat thermometer isn't supposed to touch the bone.[3]

I can always tell I've struck a chord with the collective female consciousness. The great roars of laughter confirm my hunch that we have come to see ourselves as superior to men and inherently bonded to one another in a way that we could never be with our mates. We can spend hours explaining our feelings to our husbands, laboring to find exactly the right words (read: words that won't be misunderstood or perceived as critical or threatening), then call a woman friend, say a few words, and hear her instantly respond with perfect insight.

Women have an exquisite capacity to connect, to establish trust, trade confidences, and support one another. My close women friends provide a priceless reality check for me. They love me when I'm having trouble loving myself, listen patiently to the most obscure details of my life, and are often the glue that keeps me from coming apart at the seams.

Our friendships with women are irreplaceable. But they shouldn't be used as the standard by which we judge our marriages, or as a way of marshaling support to bolster our position with our husbands. Where we run into trouble is in cementing our feelings of sisterhood through what's-wrong-with-him rather than supporting each other in owning up to our part in our relationship problems. When we play up our connections with women friends *at the expense* of our mate, we risk alienating him and we work against our own cause. And we give our friends a skewed, mostly negative image of our mate, making it harder for them to support our efforts at closeness and reconciliation.

Even if what we believe is supported by experience, the notion of female superiority is self-destructive for two reasons. First, it lumps men generically and denies them their personhood—a danger that women, who have long been victims of sexism, can surely understand.

Second, buying into the notion of female superiority can be an excuse: until our mates prove their worthiness, we're unwilling to invest ourselves 100 percent.

A RETURN TO COMMITMENT?

Despite the candor with which women report the shortcomings in their relationships, divorce rates are declining and marriage is back in style.[4] The emergence of AIDS as a life-threatening epidemic, fallout from the staggering divorce rates of the seventies combined with sobering statistics on the unlikelihood of marriage for women past the age of thirty[5] (statistics that created a brief uproar in the late eighties) have reinforced a renewed commitment to preserve existing relationships rather than opt back into the singles market.

But the fact that we're staying doesn't tell the whole story. For many of us, this marriage isn't our first intimate love relationship. We are more experienced than our mothers were. And, we are part of a generation that says we *will not settle for mediocrity*, not in our jobs, not in our educational opportunities, not in our friendships, and certainly not in our intimate relationships.

Whether this is a first, second, or third serious intimate relationship, our expectations are worlds apart from those of our mothers. Television reflects this shift. The sixties hit *Bewitched*, in which Samantha wiggles her nose and brews up yet another convoluted solution to one of Darren's dilemmas, has given way to *thirtysomething*, with Nancy throwing Eliot out when he won't grow up. In the post–what-do-women-need-men-for-anyway era (answer: semen or support, per author Cynthia Smith[6]), the real challenge lies in being together not out of need but out of choice.

We can see this evolution—from dependency to choice—in tracing the stages of the women's movement. In 1970 women were waking up to the fact that we are whole people in our own right. By 1980 women were busy exploding every sexist myth, striving for financial independence and the confidence that we could take care of ourselves just fine. Many women questioned men's disproportionate power and saw them as the enemy, by definition a part of the power structure that conspired to keep women down. Today those same women are married to those same men—men we love, men with whom we are friends and lovers, men with whom we share the awesome task of raising children, men with whom we've made a lifetime commitment.

Most women I know are serious about making their marriages work, but confused about what model to aspire to. We are uncomfortable with the outdated, two-halves-make-a-whole concept, but the contemporary model, with its emphasis on independence, self-protectiveness, and boundary setting doesn't fit either.

We are clearly at a crossroads. We have said no to the unfulfilling arrangements of the past, but aren't sure what's next. We sense the potential to develop healthier partnerships as we come to accept the reality that both we and our mates are whole, separate human beings—*both* strong and vulnerable, *both* capable in some ways and limited in others, *both* equally responsible for what happens in our relationships.

BUT HE, BUT HE, BUT HE . . .

Certainly men are responsible for having created plenty of their own bad press. And it's up to them to make appropriate amends. But we have control *only over ourselves,* which is the best reason for refocusing on the part we play in creating distance from our mates. We can ask him to change, we can state our needs and hope for the best, but ultimately, it's more profitable to work on ourselves than try manipulating and maneuvering *him.* (Besides, he'll likely dig his heels in deeper the harder you try.)

"But *isn't* he to blame for a lot of what's wrong?" you ask. Or as one woman argued, "By not blaming him, aren't you blaming the victim?" I am struck by the assumption that *someone* must be to blame. In fact, *blaming just gets in the way of having a better relationship.* Blaming ourselves is a waste of energy that promotes feelings of shame and erodes the self-esteem that we need in order to make courageous changes in our relationships. Blaming him is equally pointless. The only way to move forward is by accepting accountability for our own behavior and ceasing our misguided efforts to change his.

IF WE'RE NOT PART OF THE SOLUTION, WE'RE PART OF THE PROBLEM

After a decade of leading workshops for women, I've discovered two truths:

1. Both partners contribute to the stresses and conflicts between us (it takes two to tango).

2. If women really want the kind of intimacy we say we want, then we should stop complaining about what's missing and start working on either loving him or leaving him.

"But I'm already doing most of the work in my relationship!" you say. "I'm the one who always brings up the relationship issues. I'm always making lists of the problems and making constructive suggestions for how my husband could change."

Women are nothing short of brilliant on the subject of *his* shortcomings. If instead of *The Newlywed Game* there was a television game called *Name His Flaws,* we'd win the new microwave oven *and* the vacation to Tahiti.

We've made it our mission to be the monitor of our marriage, to assess problem areas, and to offer feedback. We think we're working to improve the relationship, but in fact, most of the time we're just being critical—analyzing him; counseling him; or demanding that he hand over the love, attention, and affection that are rightfully ours.

We dismiss the countless gifts of our marriages—friendship, companionship, intellectual stimulation, shared parenting, love, and affection—because we're so angry about what we *aren't* getting. We can't acknowledge the positive changes he's made because they haven't happened soon enough, without our prodding, or in exactly the right way.

Why are we so stuck? Because it's safer to be angry than open to new possibilities. As long as we stay angry, we feel invulnerable. As long as we expect disappointment, we won't have any unpleasant surprises. We wear our hurt like armor! It's time to take our share of the responsibility, to look honestly at how we hold on to anger and hurt and how that choice gets in the way of our happiness.

FOUR MISCONCEPTIONS THAT KEEP US STUCK

Polishing our armor leads to lowering our expectations and building a wall, which is often accepted as the "normal" way of dealing with disappointment in relationships. Haven't most of us at one time or another avoided a confrontation by shutting up and putting up with things the way they are? Haven't we opted for blaming the other person instead of examining our own role? The angry, defeated stance we adopt is, in fact, the way most people deal with conflict—stuffing in their feelings until they are intractably bitter or exploding with such vehemence that their real issues are obscured.

There *is* another way to respond. We have more choices than we realize. But our vision is clouded by four misconceptions that keep us from seeing what *we* can do to improve our relationships.

Misconception #1 My marriage doesn't have any real problems, so there's no point in trying to deal with the things that bother me.

The truth is Every relationship has problems; taking the issues in our marriages seriously, not trivializing them, is the first step toward change.

Misconception #2 If my mate would just shape up, everything would be okay.

The truth is Both parties play a part in the decline or rebirth of a relationship; we need to attend to our part and focus less on rehabilitating our mates.

Misconception #3 I'm already working hard on my relationship by bringing up problems and recommending solutions.

The truth is What women call "work" is often manipulation, criticism, and control; productive work requires letting go of all three and refocusing on our own part.

Misconception #4 If I can't have the relationship I want, I might as well resign myself to disappointment.

The truth is Resignation leaves us powerless; setting realistic goals frees us to work actively toward a better relationship.

Buying into any or all of these misconceptions keeps us stuck. Each one is self-defeating and prevents us from having the kind of relationship we want.

Looking honestly at our own part in pushing away intimacy empowers us and makes it possible to move our relationship in the right direction. And by refocusing on ourselves, we may also have a positive impact on our mate. Our personal growth and healing can be a powerful catalyst for his, and propel the whole relationship forward. As our mates witness our growth, they too may move a little in the right direction—just as when one partner changes dance steps to follow the other's lead.

Let's assume that your mate wants to keep dancing with you and you, with him. Let's also assume that he is at least somewhat open to having a closer, more intimate relationship. Why not take the first step and see if he follows? But remember, there are no guarantees. Expecting him to change just because *you've* decided to change is a dangerous setup for crashing disappointment. What you *can* do is concentrate on your own growth and healing and approach him with care and goodwill.

If, however, you are in an emotionally or physically abusive relationship, then I urge you to seek professional help immediately. Or if you decide to leave your relationship, then I hope this book will help you do so with as much grace and as little pain as possible.

Ultimately, whether or not your mate is receptive, it's a matter of integrity and self-respect to do everything in your power to improve your relationship. Otherwise you'll never know what's possible.

That is what this book is all about. It's not about sending men to the moon, but neither is it about letting them off the hook. Rather, it is about the journey each of us must take from disappointment to hope, from being fixated on his flaws to figuring out what we want in our lives and going after it in a responsible way.

What's possible when you reinvest in your relationship?

- You begin to accept his limitations and learn to appreciate your differences.

- You find that you are less trapped by the past and more able to forgive.

- You realize you can ask for what you want without blaming or bludgeoning.

- You feel freer, more purposeful, and more loving.

- You experience greater joy, trust, and emotional and sexual nurturing with your mate.

- You make clear and powerful choices as to whether to remain in your marriage.

- You have more energy to invest fully in your life.

All of this is possible, but it takes real effort and commitment. Women who work hard to examine their expectations, reconcile unfinished business from their own pasts, and give up romantic myths that fueled their disappointment report tremendous changes. They make a profound shift from seeing their mates as the source of their problems to seeing their problems as an opportunity to become closer, more committed, and more understanding of each other. They start to think of their marriages as wellsprings of creativity and support, or they leave in peace.

Part of this journey involves approaching our mates differently. Concrete suggestions for doing this will be offered later in this book. But first, we'll look more specifically at how we push him away; how, little by little, we erect a wall that keeps us alone and apart.

PUTTING UP THE WALL

Every woman's wall is a little different. Some experience it as a physical barrier, solid like brick. Others experience the wall as silence, sarcasm, or frantic busy-ness. One woman imagines herself wearing a neon sign that flashes the message *Stay away*.

"I experience my wall as an invisible force field that repels Joe's attempts to be close," says Trish. "When I'm behind it I feel frozen, locked out of our relationship, incapable of giving or receiving warmth, love, or tenderness."

Sara, an artist who lives in Colorado, describes her wall as a deep pool of clear water through which she must dive in order to find her way back to her mate. "There's a treasure at the bottom of the pool," she says. "I can see it, but in order to get to it I have to hold my breath and go under. So I tread water, hesitant and fearful. I'm afraid I will drown, but I know that unless I dive in, I'll never penetrate the distance between us."

However we experience the wall, life behind it is lonely and, ultimately, unsatisfying. The more shortchanged we feel, the higher we build it. Although the wall provides an illusion of security, it also keeps out the love, trust, and warmth we need to heal and become our fullest selves.

TWENTY QUESTIONS TO HELP YOU SEE YOUR WALL

The first step toward restoring intimacy is to begin safely, slowly taking down the wall. But before that can be done, we must recognize it is there. This is difficult to do, especially if the wall is so high and forbidding that we have lost our ability to see over it to what's on the other side.

The twenty questions that follow can help you discover whether you've put up a wall or whether you are in the process of building one.

1. Do you secretly wish he were different?

2. Do you make sarcastic or patronizing comments about him to his face or to your friends?

3. Does your mate get the "leftovers" of your energy or attention?

4. Is your relationship more work than fun?

5. Is it more important to prove you're "right" than to work out your differences?

6. Are other people more impressed by your mate than you are?

7. Do you frequently reject him or come up with reasons to avoid sex?

8. Are you more patient, loving, and generous with your children or friends than you are with him?

9. Do you fill your loneliness with compulsive eating, shopping, or other addictive behavior?

10. Do you complain about him to other people?

11. Is it hard to let go of your disappointment and anger?

12. Do you turn to your work or friends for the support or validation you feel is missing from your relationship?

13. Do you blame him for most of the problems in your relationship?

14. Is it easier for you to see what's missing in your relationship than to appreciate what's good?

15. Do you have trouble trusting him?

16. Are you unwilling to forgive him for the ways he's let you down?

17. When something goes wrong in your relationship, do you move quickly from disappointment to despair?

18. Do you fantasize often about leaving him?

19. Do you long to have a better relationship, but feel that you don't know how to begin?

20. Are you still willing to try?

Scoring

Give yourself two points for each question 1 to 19 answered yes. Add up your score, and then subtract five points if you answered yes to question 20.

What Your Score Means

LESS THAN TEN POINTS

Congratulations! At present you feel substantially more satisfied than shortchanged in your relationship. What's your secret?

TEN TO EIGHTEEN POINTS

You feel somewhat shortchanged in specific areas, but overall, you are still relatively open to intimacy with your mate. Your wall goes up when you are disappointed, but comes down quite easily when either you or your mate apologizes or makes amends.

NINETEEN TO TWENTY-EIGHT POINTS

You are feeling increasingly shortchanged, and as time goes on, your wall is growing higher. You are beginning to expect disappointment in your relationship, and are becoming less able to appreciate what's positive between yourself and your mate.

TWENTY-NINE TO THIRTY-EIGHT POINTS

If your score falls in these upper reaches, it's a sign that you feel significantly shortchanged. Your wall is firmly in place, and

your expectations have been lowered in order to protect yourself. It isn't too late to begin taking down the wall, but doing so
will require motivation, energy, and more trust than you may
think you have.

Variations on a Theme

Women who feel shortchanged admit to building a wall and
barricading themselves behind it. Not all of these women have
relationships in deep, irreparable trouble. They fall along the
continuum from experiencing mild but constant irritation with
their mates to seriously considering divorce.

   Where do *you* fit in? That depends on many things, including how long you've been together, whether you are dealing
with a number of different issues or one chronic issue that
continues to resurface, your personality, your past relationship
history (what's happened in other love affairs), and what support systems exist in your life. Let's look at each of these factors
in turn.

How Long Have You Been Hammering Away at This?

The hope and forgiveness quotient—the capacity to think well
of our partners and give them a lot of rope—is often highest at
the beginning of a relationship. Romance and sex are hot, especially if there are no children yet. The closeness created when
romance is in full bloom goes a long way toward ameliorating
disappointment and anger over little things and often big things
as well.

   As a rule, the older your relationship, the higher your wall.
There are exceptions: For some women, the keenest feelings of
disappointment happen in the beginning, when vulnerability is
greatest and the contrast between romantic expectations and

reality causes an intense letdown. Early on, couples have fewer coping mechanisms for conflict resolution and can easily plunge into despair when things go sour. Time can be healing, if wisdom grows and partners mellow and become more accepting of each other.

Generally speaking, however, women in younger relationships—five years or less—are more optimistic and less discouraged when things go wrong. As a relationship matures,

---

STRATEGY FOR DISCOVERING HOW YOU ARE SHORTCHANGING YOURSELF

Tell yourself   "I am responsible for and will benefit from knowing how I am shortchanging myself."

Don't tell him   "I'm going to figure out why I'm not happy with you."

Do tell him   "I am exploring ways that I keep myself from being satisfied in our relationship." (Or don't say anything at all.)

The risk   He will see this as an opportunity to tell you what's wrong with *you.*

The reward   You will understand *your* part in pushing him away, so that you can do something about it.

what at first were isolated incidents become deeply entrenched patterns that take on a life of their own. As we cope with the stress of balancing children, work, and everything else that competes for our time, we have less energy and less willingness to work through challenging issues. Instead, we give in, give up, and build a wall.

PERSONAL CHECKPOINT

- How long have you and your mate been together?
- When did you first notice that you were feeling less close?
- Are your relationship issues the same as or different from when you were first together?
- Over the years, have you become less or more committed to working things out?

Where Are You Stuck?

It is a fallacy that all women struggle with the same issues. Or that feeling shortchanged means feeling let down in every part of the relationship. On the contrary, women may feel shortchanged in some ways and still be very satisfied in others. Perhaps you appreciate your mate's parenting style, but feel resigned to a lack of sexual intimacy. Or you resent his limited earning power but cherish the way he makes you laugh.

Women express their feelings of being shortchanged in different ways. Some are furious about a particular ongoing issue that never gets resolved. Others experience a diffuse nagging feeling that something is wrong, much like having a low-grade infection, always being just a little "under the weather" but never quite sick enough to stay in bed.

If you've been focusing on the same issues in your relationship for years without tangible improvement, you may be feeling exceptionally weary and unwilling to try to make things better. If, on the other hand, you're currently struggling to get beyond a particular issue that's more situational—coping with a new baby or weathering a financial crisis—you may feel frustrated, but not necessarily hopeless.

PERSONAL CHECKPOINT

- What are the most pressing issues in your relationship?
- How long have you been dealing with each one?
- Have you experienced resolution with any of these issues?
- What tools have helped you to achieve compromise or resolution?

Personality, History, and Support Systems

Your personality influences what kind of wall you build. For example, very intense women may become visibly distraught when disappointed by their mates. They are prone to inflammatory statements and ultimatums, which they retract once they cool down. Their wall is an active, aggressive force. As one woman explains, "When I'm angry, I lash out with a barrage of accusations, with the sole aim of hurting him." Another says, "I imagine myself with a sword, poised and ready to get *him* before he gets *me*." Other women keep score, stealthily adding brick after brick to the wall, secretly waiting for him to notice they have disappeared behind it.

Where you've been before also matters. If this is your second or third serious relationship, having gone through the trauma of parting or divorce may affect your overall attitude and the way you interpret and react to disappointments in your relationship. You may feel cynical or cautious, or be quick to jump to conclusions, a subject we'll cover in greater depth in Chapter Five.

Finally, how much emotional support you have in your life

makes a big difference in whether, when, and how high you build your wall. If you have concerned friends with whom you can talk through your problems, friends who are objective and caring, the perspective you gain from them can help you communicate your needs to your mate, rather than shut him out. Often, other people help us see alternatives we're too angry to envision. Working with a counselor or therapist helps in a similar way. On the other hand, being isolated, with no one to bounce your feelings off of, makes you very vulnerable and more likely to protect yourself by putting up a wall.

PERSONAL CHECKPOINT

- When you are angry at your mate, are you more likely to lash out or to suffer in silence?
- Are you receiving support to help you clarify issues in your relationship? Where? If not, are there resources you might consider?

WANTING IT ON OUR TERMS

"I'm still here, but sometimes I wonder why," says Shelly, a blond, athletic mother of teenagers who insists that her husband pays more attention to the dog than to her.

Shelly and I are talking with four other women. "Is it too much to want my husband to notice me?" she asks, looking around the room as if hoping for a consensus.

"The other night Ed and I were going to the symphony," she explains. "I went out and bought a new dress I'd had my eye on for months. I was dressed to kill—I mean I looked like a million bucks! Ed walked into the bedroom, I asked how I looked, and he said, 'Nice.' That's all—just 'nice'? What I wanted was for him to drop to his knees, or at least act a little possessive and tell me he wasn't about to let me leave the house looking like that!"

Shelly's comment reminded me of a passage from a book by Merle Shain called *Some Men Are More Perfect Than Others:* "Henry Miller wrote of a young man who came to him for advice claiming he had persuaded the woman he was trying to win to take off all her clothes but that she would go no further. And when he asked what he did wrong, Miller turned to him and said, 'You forgot to weep.' "[1]

In *The Indispensable Woman,* I described how women compulsively impose our own standards on others around us: wanting things done our way, on our timetable, whether it's folding the laundry, writing a memo, or making social arrangements with friends. The same perfectionism and desire to control are manifest in our love relationships. The men we love should act the way *we* want them to act in order to prove that they love us the way *we* want to be loved. But it just doesn't work like that. They may not show their feelings in a way that inspires us or makes us feel important. Or they may be acting out of their own beliefs from childhood that prevent them from relating to us in a way that spells *l–o–v–e.*

For example, one man is emotionally inaccessible, largely because of his deep-seated memories of having had a smothering mother; another man who comes from a family in which any open show of affection was frowned on is uncomfortable even holding his wife's hand in public.

When Shelly got upset because her husband didn't lavish her with compliments or smolder with jealousy to prove his loyalty and commitment, she wonders if she's asking too much. She wonders whether it's wrong to be upset when he doesn't seem passionately interested and attracted. She asks, "*Shouldn't* I keep fighting for what I need to be fulfilled in this relationship?"

The answer is *yes*—she *should* keep fighting. It's absolutely right to fight, and fight hard, *as long as it helps to further our goals.* However, we need to clarify whether our energy is helping us move forward or keeping us stuck. For example, if Shelly's actual motive is to remain disappointed and upset with Ed's responses so she can retain her martyr status, she'll unquestionably get what she's looking for. If it's battle scars she's after, then by all means, she should keep waiting for the weeping to begin.

But if what Shelly *really* wants is partnership, trust, and true intimacy that's based on mutual acceptance, then she's sabotaging herself. Instead of being chronically angry at Ed, she might try being straightforward—telling him that she would enjoy and appreciate a hotter reaction to her appearance. She might take the plunge and attempt to find out why his response is so measured, which could be the tip of the iceberg, the outer sign of more serious sexual or emotional issues underneath. Finally, she could ask herself why lavish compliments or a show of jealousy is so important to her self-esteem.

All of these issues may have more to do with *her* than with him or them. If so, they will continue to follow her wherever she goes, in every area of her life, with or without Ed. In short, Shelly needs to take responsibility for her own feelings and for what she needs.

THE PATTERN OF BECOMING SHORTCHANGED

Feeling shortchanged happens over time, stage by stage. The effect is cumulative, gradually eroding the quality of a relationship. We don't suddenly wake up after five or ten years of marriage and realize, "Oh no! This isn't the way things are supposed to be!" With each stage, the wall seems harder to take down.

When we first enter a relationship, we are filled with hope and anticipation. We see nothing but possibilities. Even though we may be aware of potential conflicts or ways in which we hope our partner will grow or change, for the most part we have feelings of promise and patience toward any shortcomings we perceive. As the honeymoon glow fades, however, his habits turn out to be somewhat less charming. Conflicts and differences that once seemed exciting, adding drama and tension to the relationship, become more like plots out of a grade-B movie that exhaust and drive a wedge between us. As our hopes and dreams are disappointed, we become resigned, angry, and unwilling to ask for what we want. Finally, we stop believing we will ever be truly fulfilled. When that happens, we push him away and lock ourselves out of the relationship. Viewed full circle, the pattern of becoming shortchanged looks like this:

- *Stage 1: Adding Up the Hurts.* In the first stage, we begin to keep track of every disappointment. Slowly, we experience a shift from loving him to blaming him.

- *Stage 2: Building a Case.* The evidence is mounting—the relationship is *not* what we hoped it would be! We start to feel justified in our disappointment, anger, and hurt. We may recount his failings to other people, keep a mental list, or begin throwing his crimes in his face.

- *Stage 3: Lowered Expectations.* As our list of grievances grows, we compensate by bringing our expectations down to the level of our experience. We begin to disinvest in the relationship and actively seek to satisfy our needs elsewhere.

- *Stage 4: Smoldering Anger.* At this stage of the game, we overreact when he does anything wrong and are blinded to the good things that happen between us. We have created a self-fulfilling prophecy of predictable disappointment and anger.

- *Stage 5: On the Fence.* With one foot in, one foot out of the relationship, ambivalence toward our mate is the predominant feeling at stage 5. We're cautious, self-protective, and emotionally detached so we won't get hurt.

Stage 6: Shortchanged. Women describe this stage in words like these: "A lot would have to change for me to be really happy, but it wouldn't be worth it to rock the boat." Or "My anger at him is more real than my love." When we reach stage 6, we actively conspire to push him away, whether we are frosty, nasty, or simply resigned to the fate of a lukewarm marriage.

"I've got enough complaints to fill a notebook," admits Carrie, "starting with the fact that Lon is insensitive and cold—except when he wants sex, and then you'd think he was madly in love with me." After just three years of marriage, Carrie is swiftly moving through all six stages in the pattern of becoming shortchanged. If she had to place herself on the continuum, she'd probably name stage 5—ambivalence—as the one that comes closest to her present attitude toward her husband.

"It's as if I have a ledger in my mind," she explains, "and every time Lon does something that makes me mad I put an imaginary mark next to his name. When we have a fight, he gets three. Lon flips out about my 'bean counting.' But actually, he doesn't know the half of it.

"Most of the time I just stuff my feelings because it's pointless to get into a fight. I've just accepted that you can't have everything, so why worry about it?"

But Carrie hasn't *really* accepted the limitations of her marriage. On the contrary, she has mounted a fairly impressive smear campaign, complaining about Lon to her friends, co-workers, and even her mother-in-law. By building a case she has convinced herself that her needs won't be met in her marriage, so why try? In assuming such a self-defeating posture, she begins to anticipate the pattern—by not asking for things she's sure she won't get, by maintaining a constant readiness to be angry, by pushing Lon away.

Despite her hurt (stage 1) and lowered expectations (stage 3), Carrie is still choosing to remain in the relationship. But her commitment is halfhearted. Women describe stage 5 as "hanging in there," or "up and down." Carrie can't muster much hope, yet she isn't ready to throw in the towel. So she's stuck on the fence, either bad-mouthing him or playing imaginary "black mark" games instead of being straightforward about what she wants and needs. Unless something changes in Carrie's attitude, she will likely enter stage 6: physically present in the marriage, but emotionally, sexually, and spiritually estranged.

Throughout this book we will see how the pattern of becoming shortchanged affects many different kinds of relationships. And we will see how some women get stuck in various stages, while others successfully break the cycle and make powerful changes on their own behalf.

INTIMACY STOPPERS

One way we stay stuck behind the wall is through the *intimacy stoppers* we use to keep our mates safely at bay. At least some of these are bound to be familiar.

Too hurt to try.
Who needs you anyway?
Off limits.
The children come first.
A day late and a dollar short.
If I have to spell it out . . .
Telling the wrong person.
The office is calling.
It will never change!

Let's look at how each of these is manifested in our relationships.

Too Hurt to Try

Women too hurt to try may pout, withdraw, or play the martyr in order to punish him and get their point across. "I can't possibly trust him after being hurt so much," they say.

If that's the bottom line for you—if there *really is* no possible way to get beyond the hurt—then it may be time to get out of the relationship. However, keep in mind that most hurts can heal, with time and effort.

Holding on to hurt can be a powerful weapon—*if* what we want is actually to stay stuck. But choosing to remain victimized as a way of getting him to take us seriously is self-defeating. It diminishes our power, lowers our self-esteem, and does nothing to further our cause. It is a lose-lose proposition. When we adopt a stance of having been irreparably wounded, we leave our mate with no recourse. He can't possibly repair the damage, so there's no reason for him to try.

This is one area where being right is no substitute for being loved. Ultimately, it's much more to our advantage to express our hurt directly, work on forgiveness, and move on.

Who Needs You Anyway?

I recently watched a television panel discussion featuring eight women who, after numerous bad (and I mean bad!) experiences with men, decided they were better off alone. Each had suffered through several lousy romances with men who ranged from terminally boring to disgustingly rude to unbelievably stupid. One sounded worse than the next.

But as these women recounted their men's failings, beneath their bravado they seemed sad. One after another the eight women declared a moratorium on men, insisting they didn't need them anyway.

These women had made a good case for having chosen the wrong men to spend their lives with. But behind that challenge, "Who needs you anyway?" was a lot of anger and hurt. The truth is, intimate partners *do* need each other. There is a difference between deciding not to be with men who hurt us—which is a healthy, assertive step—and pushing away a loved one in order to appear invulnerable or to get back at him.

Off Limits

Wearing your high-necked, hole-ridden flannel nightgown to bed, suggesting he make a date with you next Christmas, or drawing an invisible line beneath the covers, as if your side were California and his were New York, ought to give him the message that you'd rather be left alone, thank you very much.

Women should never make love when we feel pressured, invaded, or compromised in any way. Having sex or even cuddling when we don't feel loved, understood, or cared for just doesn't work for most of us. However, we must also be honest about the ways we withhold sex in order to hurt him, express anger, or gain power.

"Refusing to go to bed with him was the only way I felt I could get the upper hand in our relationship," says Andrea, who's admittedly cool about continuing to work on her five-year-old marriage. "It was the one way to get him to see how furious I was."

When we resort to sexual withholding as a means of wielding power in our relationships we are guilty of objectifying men and denying ourselves essential nourishment, pleasure, and connection. Throughout this book, we will be exploring when, how, and why it may be worthwhile to break down the sexual barriers we raise to fend off intimacy.

The Children Come First

Children can serve as distractions, draining our energy and providing the perfect out when we want to avoid interacting with our mate. And it is easy, as we will see in Chapter Three, to become *overly* involved with our children, absorbed in the immediacy of their needs, seduced by their sweetness and unconditional love.

When we put our children first, either by consistently making them our highest priority or excluding our mate from playing a full nurturing parent role, he loses out. And he's put in a position of seeming selfish if he complains. After all, how can he compete with his own children?

The fact is, children can be equally terrific intimacy starters *or* intimacy stoppers. They are the best reminder of the love between a woman and man and provide infinite opportunities for shared tenderness. Parenthood is a great way to stretch and grow together, and with tangible results!

"In our marriage, when Steven and I are getting along well, our children are one more thing to be proud of and feel good about together," says Alexandra, whose children are seven and nine. "But in times of stress or conflict, we tend to split off, each nurturing our own relationship with the kids, almost like single parents. At those times it's a relief to submerge myself in the warmth and comfort of my mother/child cocoon, putting Fred and Wendy's needs first and turning to them for warmth and affection."

When we put our children before our mate—leaving him out in the cold or competing for the Best Parent Award—we damage the trust and team spirit in the marriage. And we set a poor example for our children, depriving them of a positive role model of adult intimacy, failing them by inappropriately expecting them to fulfill our needs.

A Day Late and a Dollar Short

Lots of men *are* changing. I see men learning to express their feelings and wanting better communication. I am impressed by the number of men actively co-parenting; it is not unusual to see men grocery shopping or picking up preschoolers at day care. But many women, weary of waiting and skeptical at best, refuse to accept and affirm these efforts. This reluctance to update our images of our mates is another significant intimacy stopper.

"That's nice, but where were you last year?" is one woman's response to her husband's obvious attempts to be more like she's asked him to be. Repeated disappointments make us quick to criticize *his* timetable. When he finally does come around we feel resentful, wondering why getting him to change has required nothing short of beating our heads against a wall (or his head against a wall).

How can our relationships ever improve if he's always perceived as two steps behind and if, when he finally gets there, it's too late to matter? If our response to all of his efforts is "it's not good enough, soon enough, or exactly the way we want it," maybe we should ask ourselves, *do we really want what we say we want?* And if so, why are we making it so hard?

If I Have to Spell It Out . . .

This is the woman who's sick to death of placing red arrows on the calendar for six weeks leading up to her wedding anniversary. She's tired of telling him which perfume to buy or, even worse, buying it herself, wrapping it, and placing it carefully in his briefcase. She wants him to anticipate her desires, to surprise her with the one gift she's secretly coveted, or the perfectly sensitive act of love that makes her know—finally and for sure—that he really understands who she is and what makes her happy.

"When I went into labor," says Carol, "I told Brad that I

wanted flowers after the baby was born. I even left the florist's card on his dashboard on our way to the hospital. When he showed up with a dozen white roses, I thanked him, but I thought to myself, 'Big deal. If I hadn't told him, he'd never have figured it out.' "

This perfectionism, combined with control, is another intimacy stopper. Women who use it are caught in a catch-22: they are unwilling to keep reminding him of how they like to be treated, how much they need to hear "I love you" every once in a while, because telling him negates the whole idea of a spontaneous romantic gesture. But they've been at it for so long, they don't trust him to come through *unless* they take over. Meanwhile, their insistence on being in control prevents him from expressing himself freely *and* it prevents them from appreciating what he does give, because they've orchestrated his every move. What a mess!

It's like being in charge of a big event. You've knocked yourself out and you know everything will go smoothly, but it's hard to relax and have a good time. Women need to stop catering their relationships and start being at the party.

Telling the Wrong Person

I have a dear friend who once was having trouble in her marriage. Problems between her and her husband would build up until she was furious and filled with despair. When she'd reached the boiling point, ready to consider divorce, she would call me or show up on my doorstep. I'd pour tea and listen while she poured out her heart. Before long I'd be totally convinced that her husband was a jerk, she was a trooper for having stuck it out so long, and that there was no question about it, she should leave him as soon as possible. Once I even helped her contact a divorce attorney and took her out to dinner while we commiserated over her circumstances and toasted her imminent freedom.

The next day, when I called to see how she was bearing up, she sounded remarkably cheerful. "What happened?" I asked, shocked by this sudden sea change. "Oh, things are much better now," she answered breezily.

After a few such incidents, I realized what was going on. Instead of dealing with her problems with her husband, this friend would come to me, unload her pent-up fury, and then feel better. She'd go home and resume her relationship, while I worried myself sick.

I began to resent being used in that way. More important, I saw how unhealthy this pattern was for *them.* Telling *me* her problems didn't help *their* marriage, it just gave her temporary relief. Nothing changed and nothing would until she began expressing her feelings directly to her mate.

Going to our friends or other people to complain about our problems does nothing to improve the quality of our relationships. If anything, it reinforces our feelings of self-righteousness. Although it may reduce tension in the short run, ultimately it creates more of a barrier to real problem solving with our mate. Complaining, analyzing, or just discussing our feelings with other people has its place—especially if it helps us clarify them—but it shouldn't be used as a substitute or escape valve.

Facing the issues in our relationship head-on takes great courage, but it is the *only* way to resolve them.

The Office Is Calling

This woman throws herself full force into the high-pressure/low-intimacy life-style of the eighties. She finds more comfort in her work than in her relationship. On the job she feels adept, powerful, and good about herself; with her mate she consistently experiences frustration and disappointment, which strengthens her desire to bury herself in her career.

Work is a good excuse to avoid intimacy, especially as more

women are depended on as breadwinners in the family. When we are expected to juggle work demands, children, domestic responsibilities, and all the other pressures of contemporary life, it's easy to see how time with our mates can fall to the bottom of the list. Work commitments seem nonnegotiable. Our husbands, on the other hand, can always wait—the justification often given by women who use work as an intimacy stopper.

These women leave notes informing their mates of their whereabouts, schedule themselves to the max, and are usually on the run. When they *are* around, they're up to their ears in projects and plans that don't include their husbands. Although they may not blatantly reject their mates or remove themselves romantically, they're just too busy, too caught up with urgent business that must be dealt with *right now* for any real intimacy to occur.

It Will Never Change!

When hope is lost, women feel powerless to reach out to their mates. "I just don't believe that anything will change!" is a cry of despair.

It's hard to hold on to a vision of a positive outcome when time passes and nothing ever really seems to get better. It can be impossible to find the energy to reconnect when what we most want to do is give up.

Despair, with its companion inertia, may be the most insidious intimacy stopper because it is contagious. Constantly communicating feelings of hopelessness, making sweeping statements such as "You always disappoint me," or "This marriage will never get better," effectively blocks our partners from reaching out to us.

Overcoming despair, especially when it's built up over a long time, requires a combination of action and faith. Trying again and having a positive experience, is the best antidote. Every good experience creates more hope. A giant leap of faith—the willingness to give it another shot, even after a history of disappointment—is also critical. Behaving as if we expect the marriage to be a source of fulfillment, rather than anticipating the worst, gives out the message that we are ready to try again.

LIFE BEHIND THE WALL

Over time, the walls we put up for protection imprison us. Life behind the wall is cold, lonely, and not a very nice place to be.

When we armor ourselves, we prevent love and nurturing from reaching us. Similarly, we freeze our own capacity to extend ourselves, relinquishing the pleasure derived from giving to those around us. Nothing comes in or goes out. The warmth, emotional connection, sexual pleasure, and sense of belonging we all need, are denied us as we alienate ourselves from our mate.

The resulting feelings of bitterness and isolation affect other areas of our life as well. Alexa, a mother of two preschoolers, recalls a period in her marriage, shortly after her first child was born, when she and her husband became estranged. She says, "Whenever Lee came close I felt like a porcupine with sharp needles. After a while, I started to feel that same way around other people, until I realized I had made myself into an untouchable creature."

Faye, a graphic artist in her midforties, describes life behind the wall as being inside a tank. "I am totally encased, and no one can see me," she says. "Inside my tank I have lots of power and maneuverability. I can run over anything! Of course, in reality, I feel horribly alone and afraid inside the tank. When I'm there, my whole focal point changes. I am the center of the universe, only concerned with protecting myself. I'm terrified someone will expose me, because I feel so vulnerable and ashamed. I know when I'm doing it, but I won't stop. I can't stop."

In fact, life behind the wall isn't really life at all. Because we are spending our energy to protect ourselves, we have little left over with which to help ourselves. We remain frozen, inaccessible, and out of touch until we realize that *we* have built the wall and only *we* can take it down—when we are ready, and if we are willing.

How do we go from falling in love to living behind the wall? In Chapter Three we take a look at contemporary life—at how the pressures we cope with daily do their part in estranging us from our mates. We see how stress, combined with scarcity of resources, diminishes our capacity to be loving and intimate.

THREE

BABIES, BILLS, AND BETTER THINGS TO DO

"I'm sure Bill and I would have a wonderful relationship," I overheard one woman tell another, "if we had time to *have* a relationship." I knew just what she meant. Most women really want to have a stronger, more loving connection with their mates. But it's hard to keep the flame of friendship and romance burning under the deluge of daily life.

No matter how much we love our mate, the combination of stress and feeling shortchanged saps our energy and drains the romance from our relationship. When we're operating from a deficit, we just don't have much left for him. We're too tired, distracted, angry, or tense to be civil. Our mate falls off our "urgent" list because it seems as if he can take care of himself. (After all, he *is* an adult!) Or we're sick of taking care of him. Or the other parts of our lives seem easier, more manageable, even more gratifying than our marriages. Meanwhile, we tell ourselves that the romance will "keep," or that problems between us will solve themselves in time.

The contrast between what's normal and what's possible in the way of intimacy is glaringly obvious to me when I reflect on vacations Gary and I have taken without the kids—vacations we would anticipate for months, as if we were holding two first-class tickets to Paradise. Here's how it went. . . .

* * *

From the moment we fasten our seat belts, I start to relax. Gary skims through back issues of *Esquire* and munches on health mix. I pull out my spiral notebook and start journaling instead of working on chapter outlines or workshop agendas. We smile at each other. We're polite. I notice how intently Gary is reading, and I wait to interrupt until he's finished. He suggests I curl up and take a nap, then covers me with his jacket.

Before we've taxied down the runway, my feelings toward Gary begin to change. I notice how cute he is, and I sense that if he were a stranger, I'd probably be interested. I feel stirrings of desire. My image of the two of us undergoes a transformation. For the first time in months, I think of us as a couple, intimate traveling companions on a romantic vacation, rather than parents or business partners. Temporarily shorn of responsibility, *we* start to seem like "kids" whose only job is to have fun, relax, and enjoy each other.

We arrive in Ft. Lauderdale, pick up our rented car, and drive to a spotless and spacious condo overlooking the Intercoastal Waterway. We unpack, go out for fresh seafood, and then fall into a heavy, dreamless sleep from which we awaken twelve hours later.

Once we feel human again, we happily fall into vacation mode: naps, sunbathing, walks along the beach, shopping, eating in restaurants, making love, catching up on each others' lives. We relish the luxury of talking to each other at eleven A.M., when we're fresh, instead of eleven P.M., when we're ragged. Listening to Gary when I'm rested, rather than when I'm exhausted and on sensory overload, is like being in an altered state.

Replenished, Gary and I rediscover each other. I remember that he loves to get up early to buy grapefruit, croissants, and the *New York Times*. I remember how beautifully tanned he gets within hours, that shopping turns him into Atilla the Hun, that he adores oysters on the half-shell, and how dear he is searching for twenty-seven seashells for Zoe's second-grade class. I remember how much I love the rhythm of making love together: the familiarity and fit of our bodies, the deeply satisfying pleasure that makes me wonder how we can pay so little attention to something that gives us both so much joy.

Each day together is better than the last. Even the one big fight we usually have sometime around day four is more fun and more productive than the fights we have at home. We're both passionate about our opinions, and we often disagree. But when we're away, we do it without hurting each other. We listen patiently, and we're better at coming up with solutions. We don't have to stop in the middle because the kids need attention or the phone's ringing or it's midnight and we're too tired to keep track of what we're fighting about.

Last year's fight was about stress. We sat one afternoon in our favorite seaside café, The Wharf, having a heated argument about the overwhelming amount of pressure in our lives. "It's your fault," I argued, "because you take me for granted!"

"No, you're to blame," he retorted, reminding me that he is calm and rational, whereas I regularly lose it, and worry myself into a frenzy.

"You're right," I said, laughing. "I guess I am a wreck."

"But you do so much," he replied, covering my hand with his. "I should appreciate you more."

Together we composed a list titled "Stress-Reducing Life Changes" on a paper napkin. We agreed to move the kids' bedtime back half an hour, switch to decaf, exercise regularly, make time for sex, and let the answering machine pick up calls between six P.M. and the kids' bedtime. We both signed off on the list and committed to following it, starting with retyping it on the computer as soon as we got home.

One year later, that crumpled napkin is buried at the bottom of my purse, covered with makeup, bits of M&M's, and the best intentions in the world. Every so often I run into it when I'm scrounging around for change, and I wonder what happened to all the conviction. Sitting in that café, staring out at the great expanse of the Atlantic Ocean, everything seemed possible. Back home, it all fell apart.

The disintegration began in the Atlanta airport, where we had forty-five minutes to change planes. Gary wanted me to have a snack with him, but instead, I insisted on spending our few remaining moments in the airport gift shop buying Atlanta Falcons T-shirts for the kids. On board the plane, Gary snapped at me the third time I interrupted his magazine reading to ask who was going to take Zoe to the dentist on Wednesday. He got angrier still when I suggested he turn down the flight attendant's offer of coffee and have decaf instead.

Fed up with his attitude, I silently grabbed my notebook and started working on my outline for Chapter Six. I closed my eyes and all my projects zoomed in on my consciousness, floating before me like cartoon characters vying for center stage, each wearing a sidewalk sign painted with a huge deadline in fluorescent colors, and singing, "Get a job, da da da da dadadadada, Get a job, da da da da dadadadada. . . ." I started to sweat. How could Gary sit there, nonchalantly reading when I was up to my eyeballs in work? "Go to sleep," he snarled, when I asked him whether he thought the T-shirt I'd bought Evan was too small.

"Skip it," I muttered back. The space between us widened as I curled up in my seat, leaning as far away from him as possible. I smiled at the guy in the seat next to me, who smiled back sympathetically.

Back home I sat on the kitchen floor while the kids opened their presents. Gary schlepped in two large suitcases, a carryon, and ten days worth of mail in between fielding phone calls from my mother, my mother-in-law, and half a dozen friends. It was eight thirty by the time we'd finished eating and ten o'clock before I got the kids to bed. Exhausted, we opened the mountain of mail, starting with the Visa bill for the airline tickets. I unpacked, threw two weeks of laundry into the washing machine and laid out the kids' school clothes.

We'd been home all of three hours, and already the romance

and closeness had dissipated into thin air. Gary crawled into bed and fell right to sleep; I joined him there, lying wide awake, wondering how—short of winning the sweepstakes and becoming permanent beach bums—we might take a little bit of vacation magic and make it part of our everyday lives.

The demands of day-to-day lives, formidable though they are, do not have to destroy the precious possibilities for intimacy with our mates. The real question is how do we recapture the commitment to make our marriage a wellspring, instead of letting the relationship become yet another source of pressure in our lives? How do we find the energy to give our romance the time and attention it deserves? How do we tend our most promising garden so it will flourish and yield perennial fruits?

We have explored various ways women put up the wall and push away intimacy with their mates. In this chapter we turn to the present—to the day-to-day demands of contemporary life and how they interfere with our love affairs. We follow three women with very different life-styles through a typical day in each of their lives. Each is coping with too much stress and a scarcity of resources—not enough time, energy, support, or emotional nurturing. Each is faced with the incredibly difficult task of cultivating intimacy between herself and her mate in the midst of deadlines, babies, dirty dishes, money pressures, family problems, and all the other inescapably energy-draining aspects of life.

A DAY IN THE LIFE

7 : 3 0   A. M.

"Raggedy Andy's arm fell off," wails Lucy's three-year-old son, Joseph, dragging his tattered, love-torn doll down the hall and into his parents' room. He collides with eight-year-old Kelly and Bryan, five and a half, who is tugging at the rumpled bedsheets on the king-size bed, whimpering that his stomach hurts and his head doesn't feel so good either.

"One sick kid and it all goes to hell," Lucy sighs, picturing her day's plans going right down the drain. She pulls her husband's World Series sweatshirt over her tousled red hair, angry that, as usual, Captain Mom has been left to cope with the crisis. Naturally Victor's off at some VIP breakfast meeting, just when she could use an extra hand on deck!

She feels Bryan's burning forehead and tucks him back into his own bed. "Andy needs an operation!" wails Joseph, sticking his beloved doll in Lucy's face.

"Mommy, I think I'm going to throw up," Bryan warns.

"Where is my pink sweater?" Kelly races in frantically. "MOOOOOOM! We're having school pictures today! I HAAAAVe to have my pink sweater!"

Today is Lucy's day off from work, since she recently cut back to three days a week in her job with an executive search firm. She had planned to get both kids to school and drop Joseph at the day-care center so she could grocery shop and make it to the Children's Hospital Auxiliary Volunteer Appreciation Luncheon. "I am woman, watch me grow . . ." she hums, dragging herself downstairs to pull Kelly's sweater out of the dryer and get the thermometer and a juice box for Joseph. She glances at the newspaper on the kitchen table, stuffs two Oreos into her mouth, and warms a cup of last night's coffee in the microwave, because Victor once again forgot to flick on the Mr. Coffee before he left. She almost breaks her neck when she stumbles over Bryan's Etch-A-Sketch on her way back upstairs.

This wasn't how Lucy had pictured it when, after much soul searching, she decided to go to part-time. The decision wasn't an easy one. She worried about losing her status in the company or being seen as not taking her job seriously enough. Negotiating a three-day week was risky, especially because she was the first on the staff to do so. And there was the money. She and Victor had argued back and forth, trying to figure out how they'd manage on one and a half salaries and still keep Joseph in part-time day care so Lucy could have a little time to herself.

They'd have to cut back considerably. They agreed to forget about new carpeting for the living room, even though the old, rust-colored shag carpet was embarrassingly worn. They tabled their plans to take the kids to Walt Disney World and agreed that movies and restaurants would be restricted to a once-a-month treat.

It was hard, but it seemed like a small price to pay for a saner life. Lucy had been sure she'd be more relaxed if her schedule was a little looser. She hoped that she and Victor would get along better when she wasn't caught up in work all the time. She envisioned volunteering to coordinate the Book Nook at school and spending leisurely afternoons cuddling, reading, and baking muffins with the kids. They'd go on trips to the science museum. The whole thing came together in her mind like a scene out of *Ozzie and Harriet.*

Now, as she stands at the top of the stairs, she can't believe how deluded she was. The beds are unmade and toys are strewn everywhere. She forges a path through the undergrowth and manages to get the thermometer nearly under Bryan's tongue. Then she retrieves Raggedy Andy's detached arm and attaches it with a safety pin.

Eighteen minutes and counting before the school bus is due. She pulls the thermometer out: 101. Bryan moans. She promises him soda crackers and a Raffi tape, dials the day-care center to say Joseph will be late, and yells for Kelly to help get him into his Batman sweatsuit. She calls one former nanny, two friends, and finally reaches her mother-in-law, who agrees to stay with Bryan for three hours.

Call waiting clicks; it's Victor checking in. "I just have a few minutes between meetings," he says, "but I thought I'd call to say hi."

"I can't talk," she says. "It's nuts around here!"

"What's wrong?" he asks.

"Bryan's sick," she begins, "and I couldn't find anyone to watch him, so I had to call your mother, and I'm running late, and the house is a mess, and now I have to clean it up, and you could have at least turned on the coffee!" She steadies her voice. "I really can't talk. I'll talk to you later." She puts the receiver down as if it were burning her hand. It rings again. It's her best friend, Randy, with the latest installment of her ongoing war with her mother and two sisters.

"I'm sorry, I can't talk, Randy," says Lucy. "But did they finally see your point? . . . Oh, you've got to be kidding! Listen, I promise I'll call you later."

The phone rings again and this time it's her boss calling to say that one of the companies she covers needs another reference on a prospective client by four P.M. Can she make just a quick stop at the office?

Running back and forth to the kitchen, Lucy brings up the Saltines, turns on the Raffi tape, and goes into the bathroom, where she runs into Joseph, who's wet his pants. "Don't worry Mommy, I saved some," he reassures her, standing in front of the potty seat.

"I'll be out in two seconds," Lucy yells to Bryan and jumps in the shower.

She makes her grocery list in her head while she rinses her hair, finally starting to relax under the hot stream of water, which turns ice cold when Joseph flushes the toilet. Suddenly Kelly is frantically pulling open the shower curtain, screaming, "The school bus is honking and you haven't signed my order for pictures!" Lucy jumps out of the shower and wraps a terry cloth towel halfway around her like a sarong. She quickly signs the release, her hair splattering it with water, hugs Kelly and pushes her out the front door. She finds another pair of pants for Joseph and starts over, struggling to squeeze his foot into the heel of his shoes, yelling at him to quit curling his toes. She swears not to buy him high-tops again until he's sixteen years old.

Lucy pokes her head in on Bryan, who's staring miserably at

the dinosaur decals on his ceiling, trying not to throw up. "Grandma will be here in a few minutes," she says. "Today was Bear Day," he says plaintively, one tear winding its way down the side of his face. "I'm sorry, honey," she soothes, and races to her bedroom where she upsets her entire top dresser drawer searching for a pair of cream-colored pantyhose without runs. As she digs through the pile on the floor, pitching Victor's dirty underwear into the closet, her mother-in-law appears at her bedroom door. She silently surveys the scene and goes off to Bryan's room to give him Tylenol.

Lucy scoops up Joseph and grabs her purse, the California Raisins knapsack, and Raggedy Andy, whose arm falls off and ricochets into a dirty snowbank next to the car. She grabs it as Joseph bursts into tears, sobbing inconsolably all the way across town to the small, white house with green shutters. Lucy hugs him and hands him over to Valerie Schmidt, his day-care provider, who promises to stitch up Andy's arm.

It's already been a long day for Valerie, starting at 6:15 when she was jolted out of a deep sleep by a parent calling to say her two-year-old twin daughters definitely had the chicken pox and wouldn't be dropped off for day care. "Swell," Valerie had muttered under her breath, hitting the snooze button and burying her head under the pillow, praying for fifteen minutes more sleep.

Valerie's head aches. A chaotic ten-hour day stretches ahead with a colicky baby, three preschoolers, and all their assorted equipment taking up every square inch of her crowded Cape Cod, along with her own eleven-month-old, Barry. She's already been up with him twice during the night to nurse. After trying almost five years to conceive, she finally had Barry, who now is the love of her life. He's a beautiful baby—funny and very sweet—even though he still only sleeps two or three hours at a stretch.

Valerie's nerves are shot. Running a home day-care center was enough of a challenge before Barry was born. She always worked hard at making ends meet and was thrilled when her earnings and Doug's slender paycheck added up to enough to afford mortgage payments. Doug warned her she wouldn't be able to keep up the pace once the baby came, but what choice does she have now? They need the money, and if she went out to work, she'd be separated from Barry and they'd just have to pay for day care anyway.

"Doug just doesn't understand how important this baby is to me," Valerie thinks. In fact, ever since she gave birth—a grueling, twenty-two–hour marathon—it's seemed as if she and Doug lived on two different planets. He acts as if nothing had changed. He still works ten to twelve hours a day down at the garage, barely lifts a finger around the house, and shoots baskets with the guys at the Y whenever he feels like it.

She and Doug got along better before Barry was born. She always wanted a baby more than he did, and he drank a little more than she liked, but they had a lot of laughs and a decent sex life. Since the baby, Valerie has turned off. She's too tired to put up a front, much less try to act like a Playmate of the Month. Everyone wants something from her, and she's tired of it! Besides, why should *she* be Mrs.-Here-I-Am-Whenever-You-Feel-Like-Being-Nice-to-Me when *he* obviously doesn't care about her.

Valerie feels trapped in her life, and she blames Doug. If he'd spoken up for himself, he wouldn't have been passed over for the promotion to station manager, and *she* wouldn't have had to take that extra toddler. She had coached him on what to say, but he blew it and acted too proud, waiting to be asked instead of going in there and really pitching for the job. She'd thought they shared the same dream: of working hard enough to buy a bigger house, maybe even having another baby someday. Instead, she's started to wonder if this is all there is. Maybe she married someone like her father after all, which is a very frightening thought.

Valerie remembers what it used to be like in the beginning, when Doug teased her and touched her. When they'd hang out at the bowling alley, have a couple of beers, and dance together. Now, when he reaches for her, she stiffens and pretends to be sleeping. He tries again, nuzzling up behind her, but she shrugs him off and gets out of bed, just as the snooze alarm goes off.

"I'd better hurry if I'm going to make the plane," Beth says to herself, reaching to turn off *her* alarm. She jumps out of bed and into the shower, then puts on her new black suede suit and Gucci pumps. She double-checks her briefcase, and makes the bed, glances at her daily planner for Thursday, December 7:

7:30 - flight to Philadelphia (go over notes)
9:30 - meeting at airport VIP club to sign papers
10:30 - flight back to New York (make x-mas gift list on the plane)
12:15 - Children's Hospital Auxiliary Volunteer Appreciation luncheon
1:45 - Employee Training session
3:00 - call therapist and coordinate with Peter
4:30 - meeting with Michael Nyes
5:45 - update tickle file and weekly planner
6:15 - aerobics class
8:00 - collapse

"Don't forget we have dinner at eight with the Daniels." Sean, Beth's husband, comes into the bedroom and plants a quick kiss on her cheek. "Please pick my shirts up at the dry cleaners, okay? Oh, and sorry about last night." Without waiting for a reply, he leaves for his office.

"Sure, honey, no problem," Beth sarcastically says to herself in the mirror. "I'll just skip lunch and pick up your shirts. Or maybe I'll cancel one of my clients. Why not? I don't have anything *important* to do!" Beth's still smarting from the argument she and Sean had last night, one of those marathons where you keep covering the same ground and the longer it lasts, the worse it gets. It all started when she tried to tell Sean how she was reacting to her promotion to sales manager. She'd worked hard to get it. Now that it was final, the pressure was really on and she felt a little panicky.

Pressure, pressure, pressure! Beth thrived on work, but she was starting to question why she was pushing herself to the limit. She wanted the life-style her higher earnings allowed them to enjoy, but felt increasingly as if she were "out there" alone. She wondered what happened to the great neck rubs Sean used to give her at the end of a long day. Now he didn't seem interested in her tensions and stress. After he quit his job at a large architectural firm, he'd turned into Mr. Laid-Back, opting for flexible hours with a small group. He was fond of bragging about how he'd gotten out of the rat race, and joking to friends about "my wife the tycoon." But he wasn't genuinely supportive in spite of his lip-service pride in her. Didn't he see she was in a damn competitive world and needed a safe secure place at home with him?

No. How could he see anything when he was glued to the football game? Last night she'd needed so badly to have a real conversation with him. Instead, when she entered the room he asked her to move; she was blocking the picture! Finally she couldn't stand it anymore and turned off the TV. "I need to talk to you about my life!" she said, exasperated.

"Honey, if you were more organized you'd get more done and then you wouldn't get so hysterical," he answered, with forced patience.

"I'm not hysterical, I'm scared. But you never bother to ask me what's really going on!" she hissed.

After that things quickly degenerated into their recurring fight, with Beth's bitterness over not feeling supported and understood matched by Sean's defensiveness and arrogant judgments. She implied it wouldn't hurt him to have a little more ambition; he accused her of being a "Type A" and suggested she learn how to meditate. They ended up in bed, separated by loud silence, and as usual, Sean woke up acting as if nothing had happened.

Shaking her head, as if to exorcise last night's scene, Beth heads for the airport, anxious about her Philadelphia meeting. She'll be signing off on her first major contracts as sales manager, and something could still go wrong. She sprints for the gate, squeezes into her seat and snaps open her monogrammed eelskin briefcase.

"Business trip?" asks a young woman holding a baby in the seat next to her.

"Yes," says Beth, eyeing the baby. "How old is she?"

"Three months today. Do you have any kids?"

"No," says Beth, "I don't know where I'd find the time."

At forty-one, Beth is glad of her and Sean's decision to remain child-free. She's committed to her career and to maintaining their life-style. She thinks about her friends who are juggling work and children and it really looks tough. Half the time they seem to be on the verge of a nervous breakdown.

"No, not having a baby was definitely the right choice," Beth thinks. "I never really had the urge to be a mother, and if I had a child I'd never be where I am in my career. I'd be one of those women people just expect less of because they have kids. And Sean wouldn't be much of a father. He's so damn self-centered. Besides, we have a hard enough time getting along as it is, without fighting about whose turn it is to diaper the baby."

ALL STRESSED OUT AND
NO PLACE TO GO

Lucy, Valerie, and Beth lead very different lives, but they all have one thing in common: too many demands and not enough time, energy, or support.

Being chronically depleted exacerbates our feelings of being shortchanged. In response, we add more bricks to the wall by:

- Investing our energy elsewhere, where we get more back.
- Freezing him out.
- Treating him as an "intruder" instead of an "insider."
- Seeking intimacy and excitement outside of our marriage.
- Giving him "junk time."

As we continue to follow Lucy, Valerie, and Beth through a more-or-less typical day in their lives, we will see how each of these five responses increases stress and takes a toll on our relationships. But first we will explore some of the sources of stress.

HAVING IT ALL—A MYTH GONE SOUR

"In the '80's women tried to have it all. Now they've just plain had it," reports the cover of *Time* magazine. Both in the workplace and at home, women continue to do more with relatively scarce support.

Two-thirds of all women who have children under the age of eighteen are presently in the workforce.[1] Despite this, a mere

11 percent[2] of major U.S. corporations offer parental leave, job sharing, flextime, subsidized child care, or other support that enables women to be successful without severely jeopardizing our health, sanity, relationships, and overall quality of life. For the most part, career women are simply expected to function as if we didn't have men, children, or other important commitments in our lives.

The picture on the home front isn't much brighter. Although more men are beginning to assume a greater share of parenting and domestic responsibilities, in most families women continue to shoulder most of the burden. According to a nationwide survey, 76 percent of women with full-time jobs still do most of the housework.[3] Sociologist Arlie Hochschild reports in her book *The Second Shift* that the average woman, adding up her duties both in and outside the home, puts in a full month's more work per year than the average man.[4]

Many women are suffocating under the weight of work, child rearing, financial pressures, and the never-ending needs of those around them. This includes women who describe their lives as satisfying and fulfilling. It includes women with highly participatory mates—men who willingly take care of their children, not just baby-sit them; men whose idea of getting ready for dinner means cooking or going out to get it, not yelling, "Honey, it's six o'clock, and I'm sitting down at the table!" It even includes women who can afford to hire help. All are struggling to balance competing demands.

But it isn't just stress, in and of itself, that creates distance between us and our mates. Rather, it's our attitude toward him—the belief that he's bound to spell more trouble than relief—that deepens the resentment. On top of all our external pressures, we feel unappreciated, unsupported, and emotionally undernourished. Too much stress combined with too little love tips the scale so we're no longer able to muster our best selves in what should be our most significant intimate relationship. Being with him starts to feel like yet another job in an already overcrowded schedule.

Not having enough money creates additional strain: We can't afford baby-sitters, help around the house, or romantic dates together that might reduce stress and enhance intimacy. We may resent him for not making more money, forcing us to be breadwinners when we'd rather work part-time or stay home with our children or at least, have a choice.

We're usually too harried and exhausted to notice what's becoming of our relationship. Instead we are always dealing with the next, most pressing item on our list—which usually isn't him. Without realizing it, we fall into the habit of putting our children or friends first. Over time, we stop turning to him for support. We forget why we need him, and search for affection and validation in other places. We begin to put our energy where we get the most back, whether it's with our kids, at work, or at the Children's Hospital Auxiliary Volunteer Appreciation Luncheon, where Lucy, to her surprise and delight, is about to be named volunteer of the year.

NOON

Lucy smoothes the hair from her face and strides to the podium, where, amid a round of applause, she is honored by her peers. "It's not often we come across someone with your dedication and creativity!" says the outgoing president. She hands Lucy a handsome lucite plaque and a dozen roses, and embraces her enthusiastically.

Her face flushed with pride, Lucy returns to her table, where everyone congratulates her. A few minutes later, she excuses herself to call home to check on Bryan.

"His fever's up," reports her mother-in-law. "I'm sorry, Lucy, but I do have some errands of my own to run. Can you be home soon?"

"I'll skip the grocery store and try to be there in twenty

minutes," Lucy promises, then makes a quick stop in the ladies' room, where she is joined by her close friend and fellow volunteer, Terri.

"Luce, Victor will be so proud of you!" Terri says, admiring the plaque.

"Oh, right," Lucy replies, her smile fading.

"What's wrong?" Terri asks.

"Oh, I don't know. It's just—Victor doesn't really get it, what it's like to take care of three kids and the house and try to keep up with my job."

"Oh, right," Terri goes on, "let me guess. Victor assumes that since you're home two days a week now, you'll do all the housework and laundry before he gets home, make chicken divine or something for dinner, and take little afternoon naps so you'll be hot and ready at midnight."

"God, Terri!" Lucy glances at the door and laughs nervously. "But seriously, I wouldn't care so much if we could just *talk* the way we used to. It infuriates me to see his eyes glaze over whenever I tell him about my job or what the kids and I did all day. And I'm getting tired of having to interrogate him to find out what's going on in his life. Sometimes I think he's more attracted to those corporate jock women attorneys with their . . ."

Lucy's voice trails off as a well-dressed woman carrying a monogrammed eelskin briefcase enters the ladies' room. She smiles at the two women, recognizes Lucy and congratulates her on the award, turns to the mirror and begins reapplying her lipstick.

WE INVEST OUR ENERGY WHERE WE GET MORE BACK

Lucy, like so many women, puts most of her energy into everything *but* her marriage. She's successful at work, a wonderful mother, a loyal friend, and a premiere volunteer in the commu nity. In the office she feels important and valued, in part because of her paycheck, but more so because she can see the concrete fruits of her labor. With her children she's loving and patient. Her friends think the world of Lucy, and her volunteer efforts are publicly rewarded. In all of these spheres, Lucy sees herself as respected and successful. Why, she wonders, does being with Victor bring out the worst in her?

It makes sense to invest our energy where we get the highest return. It's natural to spend more time working—or thinking about work—than paying attention to our mate, because that's where we get the most strokes. Or if being with our friends or children makes us feel terrific about ourselves, we're likely to give a lot to those relationships.

Certainly Victor could do better, but *it's not all his fault.* Remember how Lucy cut Victor off when he called, yet even in the midst of chaos, she managed to be gracious to her friend? As a rule, we're considerably more polite and empathetic with our friends than with our mates. The contrast is instructive:

We give our friends a lot of rope.

When our mates screw up, we attack.

We carefully respect our friends' feelings.

We dump on our mates, expecting them to understand.

We welcome our friends' feedback, assuming they mean well.

We overreact to our mate, assuming he's got an ax to grind.

We embrace our friends' individuality.

Differences between ourselves and our mates make us feel threatened and insecure.

We accept our friends' flaws.

Our mate's limitations drive us crazy.

We listen to our friends with compassion.

We try to "fix" our mate.

We allow our friends to support us.

We present a strong, competent veneer to our mate, often
brushing off his attempts at tenderness.

We have an important choice to make. We can compare our
mate to our friends, usually to his detriment. *Or,* we can learn
from our friendships, integrating what's good and healthy about
them into our marriages.

The tendency to invest our energy elsewhere is especially pro-
nounced when it comes to our children. Lucy's memory of a
botched Christmas gift from Victor poignantly illustrates how
this affects our relationships with our mates.

Just after Joseph was born, Lucy had taken the children to
St. Louis to visit her parents for the holidays. Victor couldn't join
them because of urgent business commitments. In the past, she
had always shopped for the family gifts, including the gift sup-
posedly "from" Victor to her. This arrangement had seemed
like a workable, if unsatisfying, charade, at least ensuring that
she received something she liked.

When a box of beautifully wrapped presents arrived in St.
Louis the day before Christmas, Lucy could hardly believe her
eyes. Victor had come through!

On Christmas morning, Lucy opened her package as everyone watched. It was small—maybe jewelry or cologne, she
thought. But inside, nestled in white tissue paper, was a dime-
store glass paperweight, the kind with a winter scene of people
ice-skating and little snowflakes that fall when you turn it upside down. Embarrassed and confused, she tried to pretend it
was a joke.

Later that night, when Victor called and asked how she
liked her gift, Lucy said straight out that she thought it was
pretty cheap. With her voice rising in resentment, she told him

he shouldn't have bothered getting her anything if it couldn't even be something nice!

How would she have reacted if one of her children had given her the very same paperweight for Christmas? We all know the answer to that question. She would have raved about how beautiful it was and how much she loved it. We swoon over our childrens' makeshift construction-paper art projects. Pieces of yarn decorated with Cheerios adorn the refrigerator like priceless masterpieces. But when our husbands give us something that's off the mark, we take it personally, as a statement of their inability to love us the way we want them to.

Of course, our husbands aren't children. They have greater resources available to them, and it's reasonable to hold them to a higher standard. Nevertheless, they deserve similar care and courtesy when they make an effort to please us. But instead of appreciating the gesture, we wallow in our disappointment, or simply add this experience to our list of all the times he didn't come through.

Granted, Lucy was already bearing the burden of all those years when Victor had abdicated responsibility for gift buying. Granted, his taste wouldn't win any prizes, and he could have given more thought to what *she* would like. His heart was in the right place, though. And Lucy could have chosen to see that as a positive sign. At least he tried!

Many of us, in a similar situation, would have managed a "thank you" and swallowed our irritation, still feeling the same way Lucy did inside. Whether we blurt out our disappointment or hold it in, it's typical to put down our husbands' efforts in a way we *never* would with our children.

There are two primary reasons why we place our children ahead of our mates, and do a better job of loving them: *Our children's needs seem more urgent* and *being with them gives us more back.* Let's see how each of these potentially weakens our relationship with our mates.

But Mommy, I Need It Now!

In the beginning, at least, babies can't wait for anything. During the hours, weeks, and months following birth, we literally give ourselves over, rearranging everything to meet their seemingly infinite needs. Our babies' cries are immediate and urgent. Everything else takes a backseat while we attend to this tiny, fragile human being. At the same time, we are recovering from labor and delivery, coping with constant fatigue, and adjusting to a whole new set of roles and responsibilities.

Numerous women cite the birth of their first child as the beginning of the end for romance and intimacy with their husbands. Many couples begin to unravel in the midst of the immense changes and unceasing demands that accompany the transition from being a couple to becoming a family.

As our children grow, they don't stop needing us; they simply depend on us for different things. And it's easy to get hooked on feeling overly responsible for their needs: helping, rescuing, or at least worrying about them, often at the expense of our mate, who, in contrast, appears quite capable of taking care of himself.

Gradually, we fall into the habit of putting him on hold in order to be there for the children. We may not do it all the time, but when there's a competition, we often choose our children instead of him. Instead of sharing the ups and downs of parenthood, we take our frustration out on each other or simply grow apart. When we get stuck in this pattern early on in parenthood, it continues to cost us well down the road. Being involved with our children then becomes a substitute for intimacy with our mate.

What We Get Back

Regardless of how committed I have felt in my marriage, my work, my friendships, or my community, when it comes right down to it, my children come first—if not in my schedule, then at least in my heart. No one comes close to their capacity to thrill me, to move me to laughter or tears, to inspire me to become a better person, and to make me deeply grateful for what I've got.

Marcia, a mother of seven-year-old twins, says, "I'm so much more confident and loving as a mother than as a wife, I don't know whether to be ashamed or inspired. On the one hand, knowing how much I give my children illuminates how little my husband, Willy, really gets in comparison. On the other hand, knowing what I'm capable of provides a glimpse of what's possible. The truth is, if I gave Willy the same quality of affection, patience, and generosity that I give Katie and Mia on any given day, I could profoundly improve my marriage."

For most women, being a wife is considerably more frustrating than being a mother. Our children think we're brilliant—a bona fide expert on subjects ranging from thermometers to recipes for chocolate chip cookies to philosophical explanations for why it's worthwhile to share even when you don't feel like it. In contrast, our husbands can be critical and quick to point out our failings. And whereas we strain to understand him, being with our children feels comfortable and natural, our connection to them deep and full.

Another, more insidious payoff we get from our children is the potential to use them as a weapon against our mate. More often than not, we act unconsciously, not out of malicious intent. We feel hurt, so we hurt him back by setting ourselves up as primary parent, treating him as if he were irrelevant or expendable. We may simply start out by gravitating toward our children because being with them is so nice. Out of anger—and to gain power—we soon take advantage of our primacy by sharing secrets with them that he isn't privy to. We may form tight alliances with our children, subtly projecting our anger and acting like victims, putting our children in the untenable position of having to choose sides—a destructive and damaging setup.

PERSONAL CHECKPOINT

- Are you consistently more patient, loving, and accepting with your friends and/or children than you are with your mate?

- If the answer is yes, then list the ways you extend yourself to friends and/or children, along with the rewards you receive.

- Can you imagine extending yourself these same ways in your relationship with your mate? What would be required on your part? What rewards might result?

STRATEGY FOR PUTTING YOUR MATE FIRST MORE OF THE TIME

Tell yourself   "If I give more, I will get more."

Don't tell him   "I've decided to give you a chance."

Do tell him   "I'd like to be more willing and responsive to you."

The risk   He'll reject you.

The reward   The quality of love between you will blossom from increased time and attention.

It's understandable how easily we can fall into the trap of putting others ahead of our mates. It's natural to want to be where we get the warmest reception, whether it's the kid's playroom, the office, or out with our friends. But this is a vicious circle. The more we ignore our partners, the more estranged we become. If he occupies a spot too far off the beaten path, then inevitably he will respond to our inattention by withdrawing or looking elsewhere for attention himself. If we're too defeated to put our energy into improving communication, developing partnership, or working on pertinent issues, romance will stagnate, when what we want is for it to grow.

Ultimately, careers change, friendships come and go, our children grow up, and we are left with whatever relationship—weak or strong—we've cultivated with our mates. It may not seem like a blue chip investment now, but in the long run, nothing matters more.

At the moment, nothing matters more to Beth than making it to her 1:45 training sessions on time. She picks up her briefcase and runs back to her car. Entering the expressway, she lands in a traffic jam. "Damn!" She turns on the radio and drums her fingers impatiently on the steering wheel.

Her car phone rings. "Hi," Sean says, calling from his car. "I need to know whether to make reservations for Hawaii over Easter. There's a fantastic fare if we book for two weeks."

The thought of fourteen days alone with Sean puts Beth over the edge into an all-out anxiety attack. Images of rented mopeds and remote beaches are spilling all over her afternoon schedule and interrupting her meeting strategy. She wants to be warm, but she feels pressured. Sean knows she has an incredibly busy day, so why is he bothering her?

"Can we talk about this later?" Beth says, hating the brusqueness in her voice.

"Well, the fare is time limited," says Sean.

"It's just that April is presales conference"—Beth stalls—"and I'll never get out of here without taking piles of work . . . and with this promotion . . ." She expertly changes lanes and cuts two cars ahead.

"I thought we agreed in therapy that we'd go on vacation together," Sean reminds her.

Beth lights another cigarette. "I want to, but I just don't know how I can take off so soon," she says, feeling more anxious by the second. It was a tight race for sales manager, and Beth knows she doesn't have everyone's support. She has to prove herself, and fast. There's a new young guy who's on her heels, just waiting for her to fail. She even saw him going out to lunch with her boss last week.

"Let's wait a few months, Sean," she suggests, "just until sales conference is over."

"How come our marriage is always supposed to wait?" he asks, angrily.

"Well what am I supposed to do about all my work?" Beth replies, then, remembering their fight last night, adds, "Oh, yes, I remember. I'm supposed to increase my efficiency so I stop bothering you with it!"

"Oh, Beth, I'm trying to do something nice for us," Sean says wearily.

"What would be nice is if you made an effort to understand what I'm going through," she retorts.

"I understand that you're too busy to talk to me," Sean says disgustedly, hanging up. Beth drags on her cigarette, sees an opening ahead, and hits the gas pedal hard.

FREEZING HIM OUT

The more pressured we are, the more we reject our mate's attempts at intimacy. We want to let him in—we *need* to let him in—but we're too immersed in our schedules, too focused on one direction to shift gears suddenly. So we act brisk and businesslike, even when he's trying to establish a more intimate tone. In fact, the harder he tries, the more he's perceived as an unwelcome interruption.

Let's look at what's happened in the interaction between Sean and Beth. He is genuinely trying to reach out to her, but gets hurt and angry when rebuffed. Then he lashes out at her. She filters everything he says through her anxiety, distorting it to the point where two weeks in Hawaii starts to sound like cruel and unusual punishment.

The truth is, the idea of going away on a romantic vacation brings up festering anger and fear. She automatically assumes she and Sean will not want to do the same things with their free time, and that she won't get a chance to rest and relax, which she obviously needs. And she's frightened of what might happen with so much time in such close quarters. What if things really blow up between them and she's stuck with him 3,000 miles from home? She's still upset about last night's fight and is not convinced therapy is helping. They are still in a gridlock over money, and she doesn't believe Sean appreciates how hard she works and how much she does. Most of the time they avoid each other or become embroiled in nasty arguments that leave them both with hurt feelings. At home, at least they can retreat to their work when they aren't getting along.

And what *about* all of Beth's work that she's so fixated on? Although a lot has been expected of her since her promotion, she uses her career as a way to avoid being with Sean. When relations are strained, she increasingly finds refuge at the office. She's forged close friendships; often, after work, she'll join colleagues for dinner or drinks, not coming home until late. When Sean suggests renting a movie, or working out at the club together, often she's already booked. The nights she is home in time for dinner, she's preoccupied or desperately wants to catch up on sleep.

If Beth were half as successful in her marriage as in her work, she'd be approaching bliss. At work, the goals and rewards are clear to her, making it easy to be motivated, whereas with Sean, Beth is unsure of what her commitment will yield. He's hurt her many times, and she's unsure whether to trust him again. What if she stops holding back and nothing really changes? When she feels ambivalent—which is often— she becomes unapproachable, not even treating Sean with the common courtesy she would extend to a customer.

Freezing out our mate hurts us as much as it hurts him. Beth hates herself for being cold to Sean, but she's so caught up in seeking sanctuary in her work, so emotionally self-protected, she can't let down the barrier. She wants to. She flashes on the last time they spent a long, uninterrupted weekend together. They stayed up late watching a rerun of *A Streetcar Named Desire* and lounged around eating bagels and reading the Sunday *New York Times* in bed. It was good being with him; she felt safe and hopeful. Throwing her cigarette out the window, she thinks to herself, "Maybe we could go to Hawaii for one week instead. I'll call Sean back and tell him we should talk about it some more."

"What I need is a vacation. Without Doug *or* Barry!" Valerie thinks to herself, shoving a spoonful of rice cereal into nine-month-old Lois's mouth. She feels guilty just thinking such a terrible thought. Picking Barry up, she grabs a sponge, stoops to wipe sticky cereal off her kitchen floor, and then drops the sponge into a sink already piled with dirty breakfast dishes.

She wearily escorts two toddlers to their respective cots and turns on a Sesame Street tape. Samantha, her neighbor's two-year-old daughter, sucks her thumb and falls right to sleep, but three-year-old Joseph cries loudly, sobbing that Raggedy Andy's arm is in the wrong place, and he wants his mommy *"Right now!"*

"Me, too," Valerie thinks, giving him a squeeze. The bills keep piling up, and Christmas is around the corner. Her old Chevy needs new brakes, and she just doesn't know *where* the money is going to come from. She gets up, smiles at Barry in his walker, and puts Lois down for a nap. Joseph's whimpering is punctuated by long sighs and finally silence.

Valerie takes stock of the morning's damage. She picks up the toys, wondering if the house will ever be neat and clean again, if she will ever feel like a human being. Deciding to let the breakfast dishes sit, she starts the macaroni and cheese she plans to serve for lunch, picks up her copy of *Woman's Day* and curls up in the rocking chair. She nods off, but is jolted awake by the phone ringing. It's Lois's mother, wanting a full report: How is Lois's diarrhea? How much rice cereal did she eat? How long has she been sleeping? Settling back in her chair, savoring the miracle of having all four children quiet at once, Valerie nods off again.

She dreams of being alone in the house, admiring a Christmas tree lit up in the corner of her shimmering, immaculate living room. The tree towers over a huge pile of beautifully wrapped presents. It's her and Doug's first Christmas together, and she has carefully saved for his gifts: a new navy cardigan, a book of antique cars, the new Willie Nelson tape, and a dozen pairs of wool socks. She's made his favorite dinner, what his mother always served at Christmas: turkey with giblets and gravy, stuffing, and sweet potatoes topped with tiny melted marshmallows.

In her dream, Doug comes in carrying a pile of wood. He hands her a huge package wrapped in silver paper with red-and-green satin ribbons. Inside is an elegant black silk robe. "It's beautiful, sweetheart," she says to Doug.

"Not half as beautiful as you are," he says, putting his arm around her. "Why don't you go take a warm bubble bath while I baste the turkey," he says, stroking her hair.

Life has never been so peaceful or so prosperous. Having a baby would make it perfect. Doug reenters the room, an amazed look on his face. "Look what I found in the kitchen!" he exclaims, cradling a beautiful nine-month-old in his arms. "It must be Barry," Valerie says, overjoyed. She and Doug watch as he tears open a package containing a bright red fire truck. He squeals with delight and pushes the siren. *Clang . . . clang . . . clang . . .*

It's the fire alarm! Valerie is jerked back to consciousness. The children begin screaming at the top of their lungs. She lunges out of her chair and follows the trail of smoke to a lifeless lump of noodles, burned to the bottom of the pan. She turns off the burner, climbs on a chair and frantically tugs at the blaring fire alarm.

"What the hell's going on here," asks Doug, suddenly appearing in the kitchen. Shaking his head in disbelief, he pulls Barry out of the walker and reaches to turn off the alarm.

"What do you mean, what the hell's going on here?" Valerie answers, "Just another nice, normal morning at your friendly neighborhood day-care center! And anyway, what are *you* doing here?"

"Besides the fact that I *live* here, I forgot my lunch," Doug says, adding, "Barry's soaked. I'll go change him."

"No, I'll do it," Valerie says, pulling Barry out of his arms.

"I'll change him," says Doug, reaching to take him again.

"Don't you order me around!" yells Valerie, struck by images of her father, a six-foot-four, 225-pound bully who often intimidated her until she was reduced to tears. Valerie grabs Barry and marches upstairs to change his diaper, murmuring in his ear, "Mommy loves you. . . . No one loves you like Mommy does."

TREATING HIM LIKE AN INTRUDER

Although we say that we want, need, and deserve partnership from our mates, we make it hard for them to get a foot in the door. We act (and may feel) as if we want to be left alone. We

issue orders like drill sergeants, which doesn't make us especially likable or approachable.

No two women are in exactly the same situation when it
comes to what we can realistically expect in the way of support.
There are men who are dying to do more, men who couldn't be
less interested, and men (the majority) who fall somewhere in
between. Those who are genuinely willing, often come up
against resistance. We're impatient with or unappreciative of his
efforts to take on more. Or we're too worn out to negotiate. We
think that no one can do it as well, as fast, or as efficiently as we
can. We're critical and unwilling to accept their way. We set the
standards; anything else is unacceptable. And we're still angry at
the multitude of times they *didn't* help.

Taking charge of everything—being an Indispensable
Woman—is one way to cope with stress and, at the same time,
gain control over our mates. If *we* do it *all,* we can at least rest
assured that it will be done *right*! And doing it all leaves little
room for our mates to help out, which, in a twisted way, justifies
our staying angry at them. When he won't diaper the baby or fold
the laundry or cook or straighten up or make the social arrangements (either because we've got it all covered, or because when
he's tried, he hasn't done it right and has given up), then our
belief that everything is up to us is reinforced. We feel victimized, which is how Lucy feels talking on the phone to Victor.
He's calling to see how Bryan is doing and whether she needs
him to pick up anything on his way home.

4 : 0 0 P. M.

"There's a prescription for amoxycillin at the drugstore, get
7Up at the Park Kwik, and pick up Chinese at the Imperial
Castle—I've already called in the order. Then pick up Kelly at
Brownies, and then get Joseph at Valerie's, you have to be
there by five o'clock—and if you're late, she'll be furious—
and don't forget Raggedy Andy." Lucy reels off Victor's

assignments without taking a breath. "Don't we have amoxy-cillin on tap?" Victor jokes. Lucy doesn't think it's funny. Lately, she doesn't think much is funny.

She's trying so hard but nothing seems to be going her way! She raced home from the Children's Hospital Auxiliary Volunteer Appreciation Luncheon only to realize she'd forgotten to stop at the office to drop off her client's references. She rushed to the office, hoping to leave the material with a secretary, but then her boss had engaged her in a twenty-minute discussion about another client. To make matters worse, before she left he made an offhand comment about lightening her workload by giving some of her files to one of her co-workers. By the time she got home her mother-in-law had scoured the sink and made all the beds. Embarrassed, Lucy thanked her profusely for staying with Joseph, apologized about screwing up her schedule, and invited her to stay for dinner.

"Aren't you listening?" Victor repeats, "I said there's no way I can get out of here in time to do all that. . . . I can pick up Joseph and the food, but you'll have to get the medicine and whatever else you said. Anyway, why haven't you already done it? Wasn't my mom there while you were out running around?"

"Running around! I was at my Children's Hospital luncheon and I had to stop at the office."

"You went to a luncheon with Bryan sick?"

"Give me a break!" says Lucy. "I was named volunteer of the year. I had to be there!"

Feeling deeply misunderstood, Lucy slams down the phone. All she does is give and give, without getting nearly enough back. She thought her new work schedule would make her life easier, but somehow, she's more torn than ever. She resents how Victor disappears every morning and goes merrily off to work, while she handles everything from kid emergencies to menu planning to baby-sitters to housework to social arrangements to having a career of her own, for God's sake! It just doesn't seem fair! She devours a package of Shark Bites, grabs one for Kelly, and stomps out of the door to pick her up.

Taking It Out on Him

Being stressed out diminishes our ability to know what we need and ask for it respectfully. Notice how Lucy bombards Victor with demands, which is easy to do when we're at the end of our rope. If he doesn't instantly comply, she berates him, as if he were the reason for all her problems. She goes back and forth between being martyr and monster—either feeling sorry for herself or letting him have it.

Victor hangs up and rubs his throbbing forehead. He's tired of Lucy giving him a hard time. You'd think he'd forced her to reduce her hours and stay home more with the kids! She has no idea how much stress *he's* under! There have been rumors of cutbacks at the firm, and he's trying to dazzle the senior partners by being highly visible and productive.

He swallows two painkillers and heads down the hallway to his four o'clock sales meeting. He passes Beth Martin, on her way to go over the new proposal with another associate, Michael Nyes.

Beth is ushered into the boardroom and asked to wait for Michael. She hurriedly checks her lipstick and closes her purse just as her colleague enters the room.

"Michael, nice to see you," she says. A faint blush steals across her cheeks. It's the first time in almost nine years of marriage that Beth has been attracted to another man. She didn't mean for it to happen; she and Michael just ended up talking late into the night at the sales convention in Phoenix. Since then she's thought of little else but him: his quick sense of humor, the way he listens intently to her, as if he were drinking in her words. And that intense embrace in the hallway outside her hotel room. . . . Beth finally pulled away, fighting off waves of yearning and desire.

She watches him making notes on the proposal, his elegant fingers winding around his silver pen, and imagines him holding her firmly, stroking her, making long, passionate love to her. His eyes meet hers and she knows he knows she's remembering their cryptic conversation in the hotel bar: "I didn't mean for this to happen. . . ."

"I know. . . ."

"I'm married. . . ."

"Me too. . . ."

"There's work. . . ."

"We can't. . . ."

"I know. . . ."

Beth tries to concentrate, but his presence overwhelms her. She thinks about Sean . . . she remembers how he reached for her in bed last night and how she pushed him away. He's so crude—he never touches her, never holds her hand or acts interested except when he wants to make love. Good old Sean, only interested in the finish line. She wonders if he really loves her, anyway. . . . She wonders how it would be with Michael. They could only meet out of town. She wants him. . . . She knows he wants her. . . .

SEEKING INTIMACY AND EXCITEMENT OUTSIDE MARRIAGE

Show me the woman who, after one more lousy argument with her mate, hasn't turned off her computer, put down the Dustbuster, or tucked in a wide-awake child for the sixth time in one night and thought to herself: Somewhere out there is the man of my dreams!

When we don't get enough love, affection, or attention from our mates, we're likely to seek it elsewhere. Or at least fantasize about it. Or even flirt with danger. Many wives (33 percent!)[5] cross the line and find the warmth and passion they want in the arms of another man. Whether we do it, come close to doing it, or simply long to do it, emotional and physical deprivation render us very, very vulnerable.

Sometimes we start out simply wanting male companionship—someone who really listens, someone we feel comfortable with. What starts out as an innocent friendship can easily become a flirtation or evolve into a full-blown romance. We may become involved with a co-worker or other business associate with whom we have a lot in common; many extramarital affairs begin in the workplace, which makes sense, considering that many of us spend more hours there than anywhere else.

It's easy to fall in love (or lust) with someone who sees us outside the context of our day-to-day home lives, especially at work, where we're often our freshest, most creative, and most confident. It's seductive to be with someone who finds us attractive and intriguing, who doesn't think of us as Mrs. Harried Housewife, Ms. Married to Her Work, or Plain Old Mom— perhaps the least sexy image of all. Even if we don't act on our fantasies, knowing there's someone out there who'd be game if *we* were gives us a much-needed boost and a lovely escape from the mundane pressures of life.

The less fulfilled we are with our mates, the greater our likelihood of taking a lover. Or of transferring our needs for physical intimacy, warmth, and affection to our children. Babies and younger children are especially cuddly, which is fine, as long as we're careful to not make them responsible for our adult needs. There's a thin line between loving up our kids and needing them to replace the love that's missing in our marriages. Letting children make up for what should be happening with our husbands puts inappropriate pressure on *them* and shields us from working on intimacy issues with *him*.

The fact is, sexuality is one of the first things to suffer when we're stressed out. We become like robots or machines, out of touch with our sensuality and unable to initiate or receive sexual overtures. The overwhelming majority of contemporary couples report being very dissatisfied with both the quantity and quality of physical intimacy in their relationships. Not surprisingly, stress is rated as the number one reason why.

"Exhaustion and preoccupation with schedules are the biggest reasons for women's lessening of sexual desire," says sex therapist Dr. Constance Avery-Clark, formerly of the Masters and Johnson Clinic. According to her research, which she discussed with me, women in dual-income families are especially likely to have trouble shifting gears. "Being intimate requires being able to turn off our minds and become more sensory and immediate, which is very hard for women juggling so much in their lives," she explains. The *Utne Reader* in its fall 1988 issue, titled "Remember Sex?" paints a still bleaker picture: "Do you suffer from that most natural of all forms of birth control—the kids? How about that voracious siphon of sexual desire—your work? Epidemic workaholism has even created new syndromes: DINS (Double Income No Sex) or simply TTFS (Too Tired For Sex.)"[6]

"The bed means one thing to me and just one thing: sleep," says one woman, an attorney with her own practice and the mother of two small children. "Okay, but try not to wake me up while you're doing it," says another woman, only half-kiddingly. The three sentiments expressed by most women on the subject are "It takes too much energy," "He barely touches me unless *he* wants sex," or "I just can't shift gears that easily." Yet, when we can transcend our exhaustion, our preoccupation with work, or residual anger or disappointment, making love can be one of the best ways to reach across the gulf. In the afterglow we feel softer, more open and trusting toward our mate, and more aware of why we married him in the first place.

6 : 0 0 P. M.

"Tonight things will be different," Lucy promises herself. She feels bad about the way her phone conversation with Victor ended, and wants their evening together to go smoothly. Everything's under control. Bryan's temperature is 99.9 degrees, and Kelly and Joseph are playing Chutes and Ladders with Grandma in the den. She had a nice long talk with her friend Randy, without being interrupted once by the kids.

Lucy changes clothes, pulling on the new black stretch pants and sweater Victor likes. "I'm going to start exercising to that work-out tape tomorrow!" she vows, eyeing the extra ten pounds clinging to her hips. As she puts the plates on the table for dinner, she watches the sun set out her kitchen window, a glorious pink, purple, and gold. "We'll have a nice, peaceful dinner," she thinks, putting marigolds in a vase. "Vic can visit with his mom while I bathe the kids, and then we'll curl up on the sofa and I'll tell him all about being named volunteer of the year. We'll go to bed early and maybe we'll even make love."

Her heart quickens at the thought. She goes to their room, lights a scented votive candle, and turns down the bed, plumping the pillows and neatly tucking in the corners, just like in a hotel. She hears Victor's car pull into the garage and goes to meet him at the door. "Hi, dear, how was your day?" she asks, taking the paper cartons with the Chinese food out of his hands. "Fine," Victor says distractedly. He shrugs off his coat, says hello to his mother, and takes the newspaper into the den. Before Lucy knows it, her mother-in-law has dinner on the table.

"C'mon, Victor, it's getting cold," Lucy says.

"In a minute," he calls back.

Lucy, her mother-in-law, and the children all sit down, but Victor doesn't come.

"Honey . . . !"

"Okay!" Victor appears from the other room.

All three kids chatter noisily throughout dinner. Lucy tries to initiate a conversation with her mother-in-law about the pastor at church, who's getting divorced and creating quite a scandal. Lucy tries to include Victor, but he's lost in his own thoughts. "What's the deal?" Lucy cuts in, when Victor asks for the third time, "Which pastor?"

"Nothing. I just can't keep those guys straight," he says.

"Why can't you two stop arguing and just relax?" her mother-in-law says, while Victor removes himself to the den.

"Mommy, quit picking on Daddy!" Kelly chastises Lucy. Joseph refuses to eat, complaining that now *his* stomach hurts and his head doesn't feel so good either. Baths take nearly twenty-five minutes after Joseph spills the entire shampoo bottle into the bathtub and the hot water runs out. Lucy, soaked, takes off her new outfit (which Victor never noticed anyway) and pulls on a loose gray sweatshirt.

She gets Kelly started on her homework, wrestles the boys into their pajamas, administers amoxycillin, and pins Raggedy Andy's arm back on. She thanks her mother-in-law again, says good night to her at the door, and heads to the kitchen, where she loudly stacks the dishwasher, furious at Victor who's been relaxing in front of the television for the past forty-five minutes. All she wants is a hot bath and bed, at which point Victor, refreshed from his break, walks into the kitchen, pours himself a glass of milk, and in the friendliest voice possible, says, "So honey, how was your day?"

JUNK TIME

Like junk food—convenient but not particularly nourishing— "junk time" can't possibly nourish a relationship. If our conversations are limited to quick information exchanges on the run, or we only see each other when we're drained and ready to drop, there's no way we can really connect.

We tend to accept junk time as an inevitable outcome of contemporary life, maybe because when we look around us, we see that as the norm. The average American two-income couple with children spends *thirty minutes a week* talking to each other.[7] Even those of us who put in more time still see each other after a long day, when we have little energy left. When we *are* finally at home, or the kids are in bed, our time is usually spent doing chores.

"But there just aren't enough hours in the day!" you protest. Stop and ask yourself how important this relationship is. If your children desperately need more time with you, do you find a way to be there for them? If you're on a serious work deadline, do you come up with a few more hours to meet it?

We may not be in a position to spend a week at marriage camp, but there are still many things we can do to have a better relationship right here, right now. For example, we might act a little more generously toward our mates, extending at *least* the same consideration we afford our co-workers, children, and friends. We might notice and comment on his attractive and appealing qualities instead of concentrating on what's wrong. We could put him first more often. And it certainly is within our power to earmark some special time alone with him—even a little is better than none—as long as it's genuine time, not junk time.

This inventory exercise reveals how and when *you and your mate* spend time together. Do you put aside special, high-energy time when you're relatively energetic or have you, too, fallen into the junk-time trap?

• How much time do you and your mate spend alone? _____.

• When is this time spent? _____.

- What do you spend your time together doing? _____.

- What do you talk about when you're alone together? _____.

- How is this different from the time you spend with other people?

  _____.

- What could you do to introduce more quality time into your relationship? _____.

- Are you interested in doing so? _____.

   Taking a good, hard look at how and when you spend time
with your mate can be a clue to improving your relationship. Is
most of your time together spent either co-existing or doing jobs
around the house, instead of talking, having fun, making love,
or engaging in other forms of intimacy. Can you see ways to cut
down on the junk time and replace it with more quality experiences that would draw you closer together?
   We have seen—through the stories of Lucy, Valerie, and
Beth—how easy it is to let real life get in the way of our relationships with our mates. And we have seen the challenges that lie
ahead: Can Lucy stop taking her frustration out on Victor? Can
she allow herself to soften and to assertively renegotiate the
terms of their partnership? Will Valerie let go of her anger? Will
she stop looking to her son Barry instead of Doug for affection
and self-worth? Will Beth stop burying herself in work? Will she
look elsewhere for love or start giving her best to her marriage
with Sean?
   We have choices to make. If we think of our relationships as
valuable, then we find ways to make them more of a priority.
But just wanting isn't enough. Other obstacles stand in the way.
Feeling shortchanged makes us unwilling to expend the energy
to work on our marriages. Disillusionment hardens our atti-

tudes toward our mates, causing us to let our relationships slide rather than lovingly tend them.

How did we become so disillusioned? Let's go back to the beginning, to the romantic expectations we brought with us into marriage. Who were we five, fifteen, and twenty years ago? What did we want? How did we go about choosing him? How did our romantic expectations set the stage for what followed?

I Want a Man Who Can Dance!

We all bring expectations into our relationships. *And we are all disappointed to some degree, sooner or later.* How we deal with that disillusionment—first as we give up our romantic expectations, then as we face the ongoing struggle to accept our mate's limitations—has a profound effect on who we are as individuals and as intimate partners. We may become embittered and paralyzed when real life presents itself. Or we might take the "road less traveled," as described by author M. Scott Peck—opting for personal growth and the opportunity to develop a more mature, less idealized relationship.

To understand the process of disillusionment and how it relates to the wall we build between ourselves and our mates, we must first understand the expectations we brought into our relationships.

Being married had been Julie's fantasy since she was five years old, dressing her Barbie doll in a miniature white gown, alternately playing Barbie's and Ken's parts. For nearly twenty years she'd imagined her starring role: the hushed church and the first resonant chords of the organ playing "The Wedding March"; Julie slowly gliding down the aisle on her father's arm, her gaze meeting her bridegroom's as they solemnly exchange vows, destined to be together forever. She had been rehearsing for this moment all her life.

So why was she so nervous on the Big Day? Why did she feel as if she weren't really there, as if she were on the outside looking in, watching herself go through the motions? "All brides get nervous," Julie reassured herself, shooing away the butterflies in her stomach. Weren't people always joking about the bride fainting at the wedding? Besides, Todd was too good to be true.

Although she'd dated a lot, he was the first man who met all of Julie's "requirements." She'd always imagined herself with someone handsome, athletic, and educated; the kind of man who commanded respect; a man even her parents would take seriously. Todd fit the bill perfectly. She was immediately struck by his dark good looks when they were introduced by mutual friends at a college football game. But it was his confidence that really swayed her: After the game, instead of joining everyone for pizza, he asked her out for a drink. Then, over vodka gimlets, he confided his goal of going into business for himself. At twenty-six, he was five years older than she, and already a partner in his uncle's accounting firm. He made an impressive salary and had his own, nicely decorated apartment. She shared a cramped dorm room with two other students and still wasn't sure what she wanted to do with her life.

Meeting Todd gave Julie a sense of purpose, and it all came together six months later when he asked her to marry him. She raced to finish up her final credits so she could graduate early and get on with their life together. The eight months leading up to the wedding had been a whirlwind; when she wasn't studying, Julie was busy registering for gifts or planning flower and seating arrangements with her mother.

As Julie studied her reflection in the mirror, she thought about how lucky she was. She promised herself to make Todd happy. She *knew* he'd make *her* happy; they were so compatible, always laughing at the same jokes and practically finishing each other's sentences. Todd respected her, and he wanted to take care of her, which Julie longed for more than anything else in the world.

She could see their life perfectly: He walks through the door at the end of the day, dressed in his best suit, a bouquet of white and yellow daisies hidden behind his back. He comes up behind her, his lips softly grazing the nape of her neck. She turns, he gives her the flowers, they passionately embrace, then go out to their favorite restaurant for an intimate candlelit dinner. They share every detail of their day. Todd listens intently, visibly proud of her success at her new job. He notices her haircut and compliments her on her new dress. She asks insightful questions about his career; they discuss world events, plan a wonderful vacation, and dream of a day when they will have a beautiful child together.

GREAT EXPECTATIONS

Four years later, Julie says, "Someone should take a machete and destroy those adorable little plastic brides and grooms on the top of wedding cakes!" Her dark eyes flash with disgust as she confides, "I kept the one from our cake folded in a linen napkin in my top drawer; I thought the bride and groom looked just like me and Todd. But now there's something about their fakey smiles and the way they're holding hands as if they're ready to float off the cake and into the sunset that makes me want to throw up."

Listening to Julie, it's easy to get the impression that her marriage is a failure. Not so. What's really happened is that reality has intervened in Julie's fantasy.

She feels cheated that marriage is so much tougher than she'd expected, and that being with Todd isn't nearly so wondrous as she'd hoped. She's still very attracted to him, but with time, her image of him has rounded out to include his shortcomings. She and Todd don't laugh as much as they used to and they hardly ever finish each other's sentences. When his uncle died unexpectedly, leaving Todd to run the business alone, he started working twelve- and fourteen-hour days and suffering back problems. He was almost never home, and when he was, he snapped at Julie because he felt so pressured. Once he even broke down and cried in front of her parents.

The night Todd finally hired a partner, they celebrated with their one and only candlelit dinner, which was ruined when his back went out and they took their dinner home in a doggie bag. Todd never noticed when Julie started foil-wrapping her hair, and he's yet to arrive home with flowers. She expected at least a bouquet after she called him at work and told him the pregnancy test was positive, but she was disappointed again.

Clearly, the honeymoon is over. But where does that leave Julie? Is she right to feel shortchanged or was her marriage an absurdly impossible dream from the start? Should she push to have her expectations met or should she try to be realistic and let them go?

The answer is—both. Julie's anger and disappointment are real *and* her expectations were overly romanticized. She wanted a lot, but no more than most of us dream about when we first enter an intimate relationship. In retrospect, our idealism does seem silly. We long for a time when everything seemed right or wonder how we could ever have been quite so naive.

Not all women share Julie's degree of disillusionment, but most feel that their intimate relationships have fallen short of their expectations.

REMOVING THE ROSE-COLORED GLASSES

As the initial flush fades and we examine our relationship through the harsh glare of time, stress, life crises, and other forces that test love over the years, we may feel let down about the way things turned out. With twenty-twenty hindsight and the benefit of experience, we may look back on the Honeymoon Stage as a time of innocence. Love seemed like enough, and although we may have had hints of our mate's shortcomings, we were sufficiently won over to ignore them.

Five, ten, or twenty years later, we know better. Over time we are forced to become more realistic and to discard our romanticized images. We remove the rose-colored glasses only to see our mate's shortcomings for what they really are. We realize that probably we are more different than alike. With each year that passes, we redefine the relationship, the fuzzy edges coming into sharper focus as we shed our illusions. He is who he is but not necessarily who we wanted him to be. He's a wonderful father but gets passed over for the big promotion. He's great in bed but doesn't talk to us. He's as ambitious as Donald Trump but forgets our anniversary.

As we get to know him, we become intimately acquainted with his idiosyncracies and his world view. We learn what conflicts and incompatibilities divide us. Our earlier, heroic image takes on a gritty edge of realism. Our knight in shining armor looks like an imperfect human being after all—no more, no less.

The early, romanticized stage of love makes me think of raspberries. In Minneapolis, where I live, raspberries have a short season; they appear in the supermarkets around the first of June, and by August they're gone. Each year, tasting the first luscious berry evokes the sweet, luxurious anticipation of summer. But by season's end, raspberries are taken for granted. We scrutinize each berry for mold or mushiness, muttering about those that don't live up to our standards. We may even pass them by entirely, infatuated with grapes or strawberries instead.

The same is true in our intimate relationships. The first taste is delicious. Our initial awakening to another person is filled with wonder and hope. Karla, divorced after eight years of marriage, recalls, "My first impressions of Luke are indelibly sketched in my memory. Just being in the same room made my knees go weak. . . . The other day I was rereading my old journals, and I came on an entry written after our third date. Looking back, I can see how swept away I was, so much so that I didn't really see who he was. In it, I referred to Luke as 'this sweet, gentle man who I am convinced is my soulmate.' Soulmate, schmoulmate!" she sneered. "I *thought* he was gentle, but when it really came down to it, he was weak and spineless. He didn't have any ambition and he couldn't stand up for himself. Before we'd reached the one-year mark, I'd lost all respect for him!"

Back to the Garden

Every relationship changes over time. Who we are, what we are looking for, and what we expect from our mate is in constant flux. Our dreams are different at thirty or forty than at twenty-two or twenty-three. Looking back at our first impressions helps us better understand who we were then and what romantic expectations we brought with us into our relationships.

I recently asked my close friend Jill to share her memories of the first weeks and months of my romance with Gary. I turned to her after an awful fight when Gary and I had locked horns over a relatively small, but highly charged, issue. I was feeling despondent and discouraged, even having trouble remembering why I'd married him. Jill and I have been friends for more than twenty years, and she has been close to both Gary and me throughout our marriage, so I can count on her for a trustworthy eyewitness account.

"In the beginning," Jill told me, "you seemed terribly in love with Gary. You described him as 'elegant, masterful, and highly creative.' " Jill reminded me of how excited I was when Gary and I started dating and how impressed I was by his style: his artfully decorated apartment, the finesse with which he handled his international staff as a maître d', his distinctive record collection and great books. She said I was in raptures over the brie-and-apple omelette he whipped up and served with freshly ground espresso on a beautifully crafted Danish platter.

She also recalled my reservations: feeling occasionally controlled and intimidated, concerned over possible incompatibilities and difficulties resolving conflict. "But you were truly convinced you could work things out," she said, "and that together you had the love, guts, and spirit to make it happen."

Reach back in time to when you first fell in love with *your* mate. If you think it will help, ask a friend to refresh your memory. Or take your scrapbook down from the shelf, dust it off, and look at your wedding photos or an old picture of the two of you when you were first together. Can you recall your impressions? What drew you to your mate in the beginning? Can you remember the hopes and dreams that motivated you to make a lifelong commitment?

The following exercise will help tap your memories of how you felt toward your mate and what you expected early on in your relationship. If your memories are vague or elusive, just do your best to complete the sentences. Use the *first* thought that comes to your mind. You may want to write your responses in a journal or notebook.

EARLY EXPECTATIONS QUESTIONNAIRE

First Impressions

1. The first time we met, I thought my mate was _____
   _____.

2. He looked like _____
   _____.

3. I described him to my best friend as _____
_____.

4. The first time he called, I _____
_____.

5. I was especially attracted to his _____
_____.

6. I was a little put off by _____
_____.

7. He reminded me of _____
_____.

First Feelings

1. Being with him made me feel _____
_____.

2. I really liked the way he _____
_____.

3. My greatest fear was _____
_____.

4. The first time he touched me, I felt _____
_____.

5. He was the first person who ever _____
_____.

6. I knew I was in love with him when _____
_____.

Early Expectations

1. I assumed my mate would provide _____
_____.

2. I believed that men are responsible for _____
_____.

3. I thought he'd support me by _____
_____.

4. I secretly hoped he'd become more _____
   _____.

5. I believed if he loved me enough he'd _____
   _____.

6. I thought we were both committed to _____
   _____.

7. I wanted our sexual relationship to _____
   _____.

8. I thought being with him would help me _____
   _____.

9. I expected that ten years down the road we'd _____
   _____.

As we become increasingly settled in our relationships, it's hard to recapture the excitement and optimism we felt earlier on. Traveling back in time reactivates these feelings, helping us to remember the qualities that first attracted us to our mates.

In later chapters you'll have the chance to compare your answers to how you feel in the present. For now, it's enough to recall how you felt and what you wanted when your relationship was brand new.

A Brave Man ...
A Cave Man

"I've always known what I wanted," says Christina. "My parents divorced when I was eight. My father moved away and I only saw him on Easter vacations. It was really hard on Mom, because he only sent money every once in a while. I vowed long ago to marry a man who was stable and had money. I suppose you could say I set my sights on my own version of the prince on the white horse: a wonderful man who'd make me feel really, really secure."

How pervasive is this highly romanticized image of relationships? Where do these idealized expectations come from?

Of the women I interviewed, 80 percent echoed some version of the romantic ideal that shaped Christina's expectations. Despite the contemporary emphasis on self-sufficiency, most women still hold the expectation that the man of their dreams will provide substantial economic and emotional support.

We want a man to take care of us—even if we can take care of ourselves just fine. And, in some ways, we still want to be rescued—from family pressures, financial struggles, loneliness, and lack of direction. We want all the "riches" we grew up believing we were entitled to, according to the fairy tales. With few exceptions, women who are independent in other outward aspects of their lives, continue to hang on to an unrealistic belief in the mythological Prince Charmings and knights in shining armor, the soothing and seductive stuff of our little-girl dreams.

After all, what little girl *hasn't* fantasized herself to be the long-suffering Cinderella, swept away (and vindicated) by her handsome prince? Or cast herself as Sleeping Beauty or Snow White, awakened from near death with The Kiss, that most eloquent romantic gesture? My personal favorite, from the time I first saw the movie *Camelot*, was lovely, tragic Guinevere, torn between powerful King Arthur and passionate Lancelot, nursing her broken heart in the nunnery after being saved from burning at the stake. Talk about drama!

Our unquenchable thirst for drama and romance is part of what drives our fascination with the suffering victim/brave hero scenario played out in fairy tales and movies. Even as we grow up and reject the simplicity and obvious sexism of such stories, on a deeper, subconscious level we are affected by the power of their imagery, deeply imbedded during our most impressionable years.

A MODERN FAIRY TALE

Although the Cinderella story continues to hold allure, in many ways we've discarded the image of ourselves as powerless, passive, and poverty-stricken, waiting to be swept off to the castle by our handsome prince. But we have created a new, modern myth. The modern-day fairy tale reads like this:

Once upon a time there was a little girl named Chloe. She was shy and serious, with huge dark eyes and auburn curls down to her shoulders. Chloe was a middle child. Her older sister, Beatrice, was clever and dazzling. Her younger brother, Henry, was a sweet boy, doted on by their father.

Next to her sister and brother, Chloe faded into the background. Her mother, Therese, was always flitting here and there, busy with society luncheons and charity balls. Her father, Thomas, mild mannered and balding, was ill at ease around Chloe. He took Henry with him everywhere he went, and Beatrice never failed to amuse him. But he barely acknowledged Chloe, save for an occasional pat on the head.

As long as she could remember, Chloe had wanted desperately to get her mother and father's attention but to no avail. So she buried herself in her books, soothing her loneliness with colorful pictures of faraway places. She dreamed of someday traveling and taking beautiful photographs like the ones in her storybooks. In her solitude, she spun a wondrous tale.

Someday—her fantasy went—she would become a world-famous photographer. She would travel to exotic places and on board a ship meet a man who would fall madly in love with her. He would be strong, but sensitive. Protective without smothering her; loving, but fully capable of taking care of himself. He would be worldly, at home in the kitchen as well as the bedroom. He would buy ripe oranges and avocados at the bazaar, be an excellent conversationalist, and be macho enough to keep her interested.

He would have an impressive career—something very lucrative with flexible hours so that he could be an involved parent and support them fully should she choose to have children and want to stay home with them, or take a year off to study. He would willingly do an equal part of the housework.

They'd have separate interests and meaningful friendships of their own, but similar values would cement their commitment. She'd learn about his love for horses; he'd share her appreciation of art. At times their work would demand that they travel independently, but they would rendezvous in Cairo or St. Moritz. He would buy her romantic little gifts and remember to tell her how much she meant to him. She would be his princess, and they would live happily ever after.

This perfect blend of intimacy and independence is the hallmark of many a modern woman's fairy tale. We want a man who is interested in our full repertoire as human beings, who respects our choices and doesn't patronize us. We insist on equal partnership—in every sphere—but we still want to be adored, protected, and supported. We want a man who is sexy and can hold his own, who isn't scared or wimpy, who is independent yet involved, and aware of and in touch with his feelings. In short, we want to fall in love with an updated version of Cinderella's prince. We just don't want him to run our lives.

But there are significant trade-offs to moving away from the totally-involved-with-and-dependent-on-him model of relationships, to this newer it's-nice-when-we're-together-but-I-can-get-along-just-fine-without-you way of looking at love. We value our independence; we're ambivalent about its costs. While proud of our achievements, we resent that so much is expected of us. We'd like him to make enough money so we'd never have to work again, but we'd be outraged if anyone suggested we quit. We would bristle at "caveman" possessiveness, but wish he weren't completely blasé when we told him we were going to a sales conference with forty-two men. We wouldn't be happy stuck in the role of Domestic Goddess, but there are days when we'd gladly return to a less complicated life.

WOMEN, FROGS, AND PRINCES

Whether we've conjured up a traditional Prince Charming or a more modern-day version, we use men as intimacy objects when we look to them to fulfill our romantic expectations. We put tremendous pressure on them, expecting them to rescue us or give us the love we've been looking for all our lives. As one man says, "I feel like I'm supposed to look like Robert Redford, come on like Casanova, and be as understanding as the boy next door. And," he continues, "if I screw up, she freaks out, says I don't love her, and threatens to leave."

We approach our relationships this way *not* because we are stupid or naive or unreasonably demanding, but because our culture has sold us the message that being loved means being taken care of, that romance is the same as love, and that anything different is boring and suspect.

Mistaking romantic fusion and dependency for love is an age-old theme—from the classic tragedy of *Romeo and Juliet* to contemporary hit movies like *Fatal Attraction,* in which actress Glenn Close turns a one-night affair into a crazed emotional obsession.

Women swoon in countless media images, from popular romance novels to commercial advertising. Falling in love is the ideal. These images perpetuate the misconception that *someone outside ourselves* can "fill us up," and that when it happens, fireworks will explode, bells will ring, and we will never be sad or lonely or needy anymore. We're frantic to "fall in love" and "stay in love," so as to achieve a perpetual state of enmeshed ecstasy.

We mistake the intensity of romance for the intimacy of real love. We are obsessed with meeting and marrying a man who will "make us happy." We are determined to sustain for all time the romantic "rush" we get in the beginning—a sad and impossible goal. When the rush wears off, when we face real-life conflicts or down times when we just don't connect with our mate, we panic, terrified that love's time is up, like a flickering light bulb about to burn out. Our focus on maintaining romantic fusion keeps us from recognizing the opportunity for something deeper. And that is real love, that which comes from deeply knowing and accepting another person, holding fast on the day-to-day journey of life with our intimate partner.

It's like trying to appreciate the taste of cool, pure water when we're used to the heady zing of champagne. The truth is, we couldn't take intense romance as a steady diet any more than we could drink Dom Pérignon at every meal. Instead of enjoying the initial thrill of infatuation and accepting, even rejoicing in its eventual shift to a softer, quieter kind of love and commitment, we keep trying to recapture what was.

As long as we cling to the hope that one day our prince will come, we stunt our own growth and the potential for true partnership. Says Stephanie Covington, author of *Leaving the Enchanted Forest: The Path from Relationship Addiction to Intimacy,* "As women, we have accepted the notion that if only we *find the right person* [italics mine] we'll fall in love and live happily ever after—as fairy tales promise."[1]

Although fairy tales create the original backdrop against which we develop our romantic expectations, for me, and for many women growing up at the time I did, it was the articles in teen and women's magazines that fueled my fantasies of falling in love.

Articles like these from *Cosmopolitan* filled my waking hours: "38 Men Tell a Nice Girl Like You What Turns Them on," "How to Be His Last Wife," and "How to Have Rich Girl Hair." I was starved for information, and I saved my allowance, greedily perusing the racks at Sol's Superette, speed-reading down tables of contents, deciding which magazines each month offered the most promising advice. Those magazines—*Seventeen, Cosmopolitan,* and *Glamour*—gave me a glimpse of what was possible, *if* I wrapped my hair in orange juice cans, made witty small talk, and wore the right shade of lipstick (Yardley's "strawberry mist" gloss circa 1970). I spent hours lying in bed, drinking in every word, searching for the magic answer that would reveal what I needed to get and keep the boy of my dreams. Between the ages of thirteen and seventeen, most of my time was spent utterly preoccupied with the promises projected in those magazines, which I read as if they were scripture.

Those promises—and the expectations they created—were of Perfect Romance. The magazine publishers sold (and I bought) the belief that having a boyfriend, fiancé, or husband was every girl's goal in life. And they told me that by fulfilling that goal, I would fulfill my potential as a person.

Even at age fifteen, when I met Martin, my first love, I had other ambitions in life besides finding a boyfriend. My friendships were terribly important, and I always knew I'd have a career. But nothing compared in intensity and importance to the first kiss; the first ID bracelet; or the first time I spoke the words *my boyfriend,* swollen with pride and ownership. Being part of a pair superseded anything I could do by myself.

Throughout my teens, the articles, along with the music of the times (which compared love with everything from a heatwave to an incurable disease) profoundly affected my romantic expectations and continued to do so for the next two decades. Today, when something isn't right in my marriage, I still wonder if it's really because my hair doesn't look good or I'm wearing the wrong outfit. I still think in terms of how I can get him to love me more. I still feel entitled to have my expectations met, and when they're not, I question our compatibility, my commitment, and whether it's worth it to keep on trying.

Holding on to our romantic expectations keeps us banging our heads against the wall, trying to *get* something that's unattainable. Like a young child who struggles to put a square peg in a round hole, our efforts to "make" our relationships work through sheer will, combined with the false belief that we can control our mates' responses, are sure to result in failure. The child with the toy believes in his omnipotent power to manipulate the world to his liking. Similarly, we engage in magic thinking, constructing a fantasy world where we hope and pray for our mate to fulfill our expectations. We keep waiting for him to assume his princely grace, convinced that when he does we will be happy forevermore.

Personal Checkpoint

- Describe your fantasy of the Perfect Relationship.
- Do you know where your fantasy comes from—books, magazines, television, movies . . . ?
- How does your present relationship compare to your romantic fantasy?

Explicit Expectations and Underlying Agendas

The quality of our relationships is always measured against our expectations. When we feel disappointed, it's useful to ask ourselves, "Is there some expectation of mine that isn't being met?" or "What do I want that I'm not getting?" When our expectations are met, we are content and rate our relationship as successful. Conversely, the degree to which we are thwarted dictates how hurt or angry we feel.

Expectations work in one of two ways: They can be useful

tools for clarifying what we want or they can be instruments of manipulation and control. Here is the distinction: *Knowing what we want is vital to having a better relationship; expecting our mate to automatically satisfy those desires is unrealistic and leads to trouble.*

We bring two kinds of expectations into our intimate relationships: *explicit expectations*—what we consciously wish and hope for; and *underlying agendas*—the unconscious needs we project onto our partner. Examples of explicit expectations are "I want a man who can dance" or "I'll never marry someone who drinks like my father did." Examples of underlying agendas are "He will give me the nurturing I never got as a child" or "Finally there is someone who will protect me from the world." Chapter Five focuses on underlying agendas. Here, we will look closely at explicit expectations and how they color our lives.

Unless we really *are* married to The Perfect Man, our expectations will clash with reality and we are bound to be let down. When this happens, we may react in various ways:

- We may question what attracted us in the first place and fantasize about getting our needs met elsewhere.

- We may fight the changes in our relationship, hiding behind our anger and hurt, and decide we have been sold a bill of goods.

- We may adapt and learn to live with and appreciate who he is, flaws and all.

ONE-WAY CONTRACTS

Our explicit expectations are expressed in our relationships as *one-way contracts*. They are one-way, rather than mutual, because *we* know what we're after, but we don't necessarily communicate this to our mate.

One-way contracts are almost always secret, and they usually go something like this: "I will care for you *if*. . ." For example, a woman may approach her husband with the secret contract: "I will love you *if* you give me the affection and attention I crave" or "I will remain committed to you *as long as* you make me feel special."

One-way contracts are different from direct deals, which we also make with our mates. For instance, commitments spelling out the terms of financial support or parenting responsibilities are deliberate arrangements that both parties sign off on. His agreement to have a baby with you because it's the most important thing in your life, and your consent to move to another city because it's important to his career, are out-in-the-open understandings. They express our stated or obvious interests. One-sided contracts, on the other hand, express our *hidden expectations.*

FANTASIES: THE DOORWAY TO OUR HIDDEN EXPECTATIONS

Our secret one-sided contracts are typically expressed through fantasies. Like the imaginary friends children invent to fulfill their needs for companionship, understanding, or security, we develop perfect fantasies of how we wish life could be with our husbands. These translate into actual scenarios we carry around in our heads.

Most fantasies are very specific. They include scenery, mood, motivations, and exact lines for each character. We create different episodes for different life situations. We may have one for romance, one for parenting, and another that expresses our idealized image of how we communicate with our mates.

Lisa reveals three of her fantasies:

Fantasy 1: And Then Our Eyes Met

T H E   S C E N E

A secluded cabin on Cape Cod. It is early October and the leaves are turning. Lisa sits staring into the fireplace, her face lit by the flames. Enter stage left Daniel, her husband, who appears agitated.

LISA: I finally understand what I must do.

DANIEL (*sitting down beside her*): Please don't do anything without hearing me out.

(*Long, pregnant pause.*)

DANIEL: I know I haven't been really present in our relationship. I've been scared. I understand how you must feel, and I know it will take time, but I love you.

(*Lisa turns to Daniel. For the first time in years, they look directly into each other's eyes.*)

Fantasy 2: At the Market

T H E   S C E N E

A trendy gourmet market. Lisa and Daniel are arguing over which organic apples to buy when they run into Lisa's boss, who asks when she's coming back to work full-time. Mindy, their fourteen-month-old, gets into the yogurt-covered raisins, stuffs handfuls into her mouth, and spills them all over the floor.

LISA (*frantically gesturing toward Mindy*): Daniel, can you please . . .

(*Daniel cleans up the yogurt-covered raisins, picks up Mindy, and shakes Lisa's boss's hand. Mindy, sick from all the raisins, starts crying.*)

DANIEL (*heading for the door*): Nice to see you, John. Lisa, honey, why don't I take Mindy for a walk while you two catch up?

Fantasy 3: If You Could Read My Mind

THE SCENE

It is nighttime. Lisa and Daniel are sitting at the kitchen table, drinking tea and talking about the fight Lisa just had with her mother. Lisa is terribly upset; Daniel is calm and comforting.

DANIEL: I'm not sure I've ever seen you this upset about your mother.

LISA: I'm really hurt by what she said to me.

DANIEL: I understand.

LISA (*putting her head down and crying*): "I'm so confused. What should I do?

DANIEL (*taking Lisa's hand in his*): Whatever you decide, you know I'll support you.

All our fantasies are *imaginary* and, therefore, difficult to stage in real life. They reflect our hopes and dreams, but only in a one-dimensional way that doesn't take our mate's real feelings and responses into account. We are playwright, director, and leading lady of our fantasies; he, on the other hand, may not even know he got the part, yet we expect him to step in on cue and deliver his lines perfectly.

We may spend hours getting ready for a special night out with our mate—arranging child care, dressing up, and getting in the mood for romance. We know exactly how we want the night to go. We want him to make all the right moves, preferably something straight out of *Casablanca*.

Or we may have waited all day to tell him about a complicated problem we solved at work, imagining him being terribly attentive and impressed by our business savvy and skill. When he forgets to notice how beautiful we look or seems distracted while listening to the fascinating details of our career, we stick to our fantasies and expect him to fall into character—and we are doomed to disappointment.

FOUR REASONS WHY EXPECTATIONS ARE IMPOSSIBLE SETUPS

It's hard to give up unrealistic expectations because they're so closely tied to our feelings. For example, we feel insecure, so we expect our mate to reassure us. Or we feel sad, so we expect him to comfort us. There's nothing wrong with our feelings, or with expressing them, but that doesn't necessarily mean our expectations will be met.

Now it's time to draw the line between expectations and feelings. In a nutshell, *all feelings are valid.* But when we convert our feelings into *inappropriate expectations*—like expecting our mates to make us feel happier, safer, or more secure, we are out of bounds.

All inappropriate expectations damage our relationships because:

1. They are based on illusion rather than reality.
2. They assume we can control our mates' responses.

3. They are one sided.

4. They limit what's possible in our relationships.

Let's take a closer look at each of these reasons.

1. *They are based on illusion rather than reality.* When we project our needs onto another person and believe that he can make us happy, we are setting ourselves up for heartbreak. *You and you alone* are responsible for your state of mind. He may at various points provide pleasure, comfort, and companionship, but ultimately your happiness is in your own hands.

2. *They assume we can control our mate's responses.* When we approach him with a request, we know that his answer may be "Yes," "No," "I don't understand," or "I'll see what I can do." Projecting our expectations without considering what he wants, needs, or is capable of giving is a guaranteed recipe for disappointment. You have no control over what he does or doesn't do.

3. *They are one sided.* When two partners make a contract and shake on it, each is responsible for carrying out his or her end of the deal. Expectations, on the other hand, are settled inside one person's head. The terms are negotiated on one side only, with the other partner left in the dark, incapable of fulfilling his part—unless he just happens, coincidentally, to say or do the right thing.

4. *They limit what's possible in our relationships.* When we are driven by our expectations, we lose the capacity to be surprised and delighted by our mate. When he's pressured to live up to preconceived notions of what we need and want, it restricts our ability to react to him in the present and appreciate what he *does* have to give.

Karen's Story

Karen is a successful trial attorney who has been in marriage counseling for six months. She wants to improve her marriage, but she keeps getting trapped by her inappropriate expectations and how she expresses them to her husband, Don.

"For the longest time I thought that if I just knew what to expect in my relationship, did a good enough job of communicating, and then stuck to my guns, I'd get what I want," she says. "Not only do I pride myself on having a direct line both to my feelings *and* Don's—I think I know him better than he knows himself. When he doesn't cough up the appropriate response, or when he has the nerve to get angry at *me* for pressuring him, I get self-righteous and angry.

"I can't count the number of times he's backed away, claiming he's sick and tired of being on the receiving end of my expectations, all the while insisting that he'd be glad to consider anything presented in the form of a request. He keeps saying that *my* feelings have nothing to do with *him*, that I refuse to take into account how he's feeling.

"Don will call in the middle of the afternoon just to check in and say hi. If I'm having a bad day at work, or am worried about one of the kids, he gets the brunt of it. After subjecting him to a rundown of my problems, I expect him to provide brilliant analysis, answers, and all the reassurance and comfort in the world. I don't think about how his day is going, and whether he happens to have two minutes or two hours to engage with me, I just dump!"

Karen's expectations are clearly a destructive force in her relationship with Don. If he can't solve her problems or doesn't adopt exactly the empathetic tone she's looking for, she gets furious. If he tries to extricate himself politely or suggests she wait or work out her problems on her own, he's automatically labeled the villain. It's virtually impossible for him to support her, *in his own way*. The weight of her disappointment leaves him so pressured and put off that he retreats. He's so sick of the message that what he has to give isn't good enough, he's stopped giving much at all.

What happens if Karen backs off and allows Don to give what he can, in whatever way is natural and authentic? How does their interaction change if Don listens carefully to Karen's feelings and is as forthcoming as possible, while still honoring his own boundaries? Consider the following scenario.

Don calls in the middle of the afternoon to say hi. Karen's having a bad day at work; she's had a run-in with Helen, a co-worker, and decided to talk to her supervisor about it. Now she is anxious about whether she should have worked it out herself. Instead of barreling in with her story, describing every gory detail like a war correspondent, she instead says, "Don, do you have a minute? I'd like to talk to you about what just happened with Helen."

Don, knowing he only has ten minutes before his next client arrives, replies, "Sure, honey, but I only have five minutes." Karen, respectful of Don's time commitments, gives a condensed version of what transpired, coming right to the point. She asks Don for feedback on whether he thinks she did the right thing in involving her supervisor.

"That's a tough one," he replies. "I can see why you're anxious." He has acknowledged her feelings. Then he throws the ball back in her court, asking, "Is there anything that would help you feel less worried?"

Karen thinks for a minute, then says, "Well, I could tell Helen I spoke to Justin about it, and see how she'd feel about the three of us trying to work it out together."

"Give it a shot," says Don. "Call me back later and let me know how it works out."

In this scenario, both Karen and Don's needs are respected. She feels heard, and he feels good about his role in helping his wife on his terms. Don gives what he can, instead of being subjected to Karen's unrealistic expectation that he should magically make her feelings of anxiety disappear.

FEELINGS VERSUS EXPECTATIONS

Deep down inside, most of us know that some of our expectations are unreasonable, one-sided, and unfair. Yet we can't let them go. We have convinced ourselves that we are *entitled* to have our needs met, just because we know what we feel and we know what we want!

Denise, forty, is a graduate of an assertiveness training course. "Going to my women's group and learning that I had the right to my feelings and expectations was the first time I ever felt like I had some power in my relationships. It was exhilarating!"

Knowing and naming feelings is critical to developing self-esteem. However, Denise is making one unfortunate mistake. Notice how she lumps together "feelings" and "expectations," as if they should be addressed the same way. In fact, they cannot be.

Nan, twenty-nine, a soft-spoken Southerner who recently celebrated her first anniversary, also has problems differentiating between feelings and expectations. "I'm just beginning to get comfortable being vulnerable and telling Ned how I really feel," she says. "I get lonely being so far away from my family and sometimes I'll tell Ned, hoping he'll put his arms around me or talk to me about his own feelings. I guess I just assume that because I'm always willing to listen to what's going on with him, he'll do the same for me. Sometimes he does, but most of the time he just sits there looking like he'd rather be anywhere else. I feel like I'm bothering him. I keep talking and talking until I get embarrassed that I even brought it up."

Here is how Nan's feelings translate into expectations:

FEELING	EXPECTATION
I'm lonely.	Ned should hold me.
I'm scared.	It's up to Ned to make me feel safe.
I'm anxious.	If Ned shared my feelings, I'd calm down.

Imagine what might happen if Nan approached Ned directly and respectfully, and asked for what she wants. For example, she might try saying, "Ned, I'm homesick and lonely, please hold me for a minute" or "I'd really like it if we could talk about having to live so far away from my family." Instead, she expects him to anticipate her needs and fulfill them in very specific ways. She expects him to play out his part in her script. It bothers her that Ned doesn't automatically know what she wants. If she had her druthers, he'd want exactly the same things she does! Nan feels shortchanged because Ned's love for her doesn't translate into reading her mind.

PERSONAL CHECKPOINT

- List the first three feelings you are aware of in relation to your mate.

- Next to each feeling, write down the expectations aroused. You might begin with the words "I feel alone. I need to talk" or "I feel scared. I need to be held."

- Make a commitment to notice each time you express your feelings to your mate in the form of an expectation.

Until we are able to let go of our inappropriate expectations, we will continue to set up ourselves and our mates. Does that mean we have no right to expect anything of him? That it's our job to become totally self-sufficient, serene as Buddha, perfectly loving at all times, regardless of whether or not our needs are met? No! The goal is to create realistic expectations and express them respectfully.

THE MAGIC OF ASKING

There's an axiom that every good salesperson knows: You have to ask for the sale. We can push and persuade, but we won't get what we want unless we come right out and ask for it.

We expend a great deal of energy selling our mate on what we deserve, seldom making a direct request. Instead of assuming or demanding that our expectations will be met, *we can learn to ask for what we want.* This simple strategy vastly increases our chances of having a successful intimate relationship.

Knowing what we want and negotiating for it is perfectly appropriate. But when our *wants* turn into *needs,* and we become desperately attached to them, believe we are entitled to them, and convince ourselves that without them we will be miserable, we end up working against ourselves. Ironically, the more desperately we cling to our needs, the less likely we are to get them met.

In his book *A New Guide to Rational Living,* Albert Ellis proposes that we can change our emotional experience by altering the way we think. He writes, "When clients claim, 'I *need* love!' we attempt to get them to say instead, 'I *want* love very much, but I do not absolutely *need* it and can survive and feel reasonably happy without it.' "[2]

Consider, for example, "love," "closeness," and "security." When we want these things and label them *needs,* we load them with an urgency that compels us to act as if life would be unlivable without them. Believing we *need* them makes us feel as if we have no choice in the matter—we *must* get them and have them, or else! Reframing these statements as *wants* puts them into proper perspective and dilutes their power. We know that life will go on whether we get them or not.

NEGOTIATING—A POWERFUL TOOL

If we need something, and we expect our mate to provide it, what happens if he can't or won't or doesn't even know what we're talking about? What if instead we make a request?

Knowing that we can live without whatever it is we're asking for, even if we want it very much, is good for us and good for our mate. We feel less desperate, he feels less pressured and less defensive if he can't deliver. The entire encounter has a much better chance of success.

"But aren't there some things I should absolutely expect from my husband, like accountability and a responsible financial attitude and a certain amount of warmth, communication, and love?" you might ask. Absolutely! If you ask for what you want and your mate agrees to his part of the bargain, by all means he ought to come through. And if he doesn't, you have every right to be disappointed and angry. But that doesn't mean it's hopeless. You might renegotiate your agreement or clarify again exactly what you're asking for.

For instance, your mate agrees to be responsible for dinner twice a week. But when it comes to his turn, he either "forgets" or can't figure how the stove works or is stymied when he can't find any ketchup in the refrigerator. (By this time you've worked harder assisting him than if you'd done it yourself.) You still have a number of options. You can remind him of your agreement and make sure you're on the same wavelength, i.e., that he's agreed to make sure every week, twice a week, at a reasonable hour, some semblance of a meal will be on the table that *he* has produced himself. You can rework your contract by doing a little menu planning with him, suggesting frozen food, take out, or other easily manageable choices. Or you can simply restate the agreement, step out of the way, and eat large, healthy lunches on days when he's responsible for dinner.

What if he still fails to keep his part of the bargain? When it's his turn, the dinner hour arrives, you're starving, and invariably you have to resort to opening a can of soup. Or two months into the deal he's still suggesting a romantic dinner for two at Burger King or McDonald's.

In that case, reconsider whether what you're asking for

makes sense. In other words, no matter how nicely you ask, or how patient you are, he just may not be able to give you what you want.

He may never be James Beard; for that matter, he may not be the guy next door who works all day but still manages to take turns with *his* wife, even if he just sets the table and cuts up the frozen pizza. If that's who he is, and he's not willing to change, you might as well work on accepting reality. Your best bet is to try to see him as clearly as possible, be realistic about what he can and can't, is and isn't willing to do, and within those parameters, decide what's possible.

"I get all wound up wanting Ivan to initiate deep, meaningful conversations about his feelings, and instead he just clams up," says Reesa. "I keep being angry and hurt about this, interpreting it as more evidence of our basic incompatibility."

I suggest to Reesa that she calmly ask Ivan if he'd be willing to talk about his feelings on a particular subject for fifteen minutes on Monday night. If he says no, then she might tell him why this is so important to her, noting that they're two different people with two very different styles of expression.

Reesa might try some creative alternatives, suggesting to Ivan that he write about his feelings in a journal, or asking him if there's another way he'd be more comfortable communicating. If he still won't, then she has to determine how crucial this kind of communication is to her idea of intimacy. Can she continue to be married to a man who won't share his deeper feelings?

If you reach such a serious point in your relationship, be sure to put your positive feelings about him into the equation as well. Remember: The goal is to adjust your expectations—and know your bottom line, which we'll work on later in this book—so you'll have *more* of what you want. *All* of what you want is not a realistic goal.

Negotiating an agreement, rather than holding on to one-sided expectations, is an important tool to get more of what you want in your relationship. Negotiations empower us, whereas expectations keep us dependent on our partner's willingness and ability to meet our needs. Negotiations offer both partners the right to make commitments and be honest about what they are and are not willing to do.

Here are some of the essential differences between expectations and negotiations:

Expectations are one sided.

Negotiations are two sided.

Expectations are rigid.

Negotiations are fluid and flexible.

Expectations are communicated as demands.

Negotiations are expressed as desires.

Expectations are controlling.

Negotiations are collaborative.

Expectations result in feelings of isolation.

Negotiations are nurturing and healing.

STRATEGY FOR TRANSFORMING EXPECTATIONS INTO NEGOTIATIONS.

Tell yourself "I have the right to *ask* for everything I want."

Don't tell him "I'm working on a list of negotiable demands."

Do tell him "These are some things I'd like in our relationship." (Keep your list short.) "How do you feel about it?"

The risk He'll suspect this is your newest campaign to change *him.*

The reward Getting more of what you want.

In Chapter Nine, "Making Overtures," specific techniques for negotiating are outlined that will help you most effectively approach your mate in asking for what you want.

Patrice's Story

Patrice, thirty-five, tells how she finally figured out how to transform her expectations into negotiations.

"I kept telling Mark over and over that I was starving for more intimacy from him, but nothing I said seemed to make any difference. 'You want me to be someone else,' he'd say. 'That's not my style!' For months all we did was argue. Whenever I was

with him I felt lonely, as if he just didn't want to understand me.
I kept trying to explain. I needed him to be warmer, to really
connect with me, but the more I talked, the more he moved
away. When I wasn't with him I spent plenty of time brooding or
plotting my dramatic exit from our marriage if things didn't
change."

What finally did change was Patrice's understanding of
what it means to be respectful and responsible in her relationship. "One day Susan, a friend of mine, confronted me on all the
steam I was blowing off about Mark," she explains. "She put her
hand on mine and said, 'What you want is really okay, Pat, but
you don't believe it. Maybe that's why you keep laying all your
disappointment on Mark, I think he could be more open if you'd
figure out just what it is you want him to *do* and ask him in a
nice way.

"I started crying! I realized that what I wanted was simply
for Mark to do two things: to touch me more—not sexually, but
tenderly—and occasionally to ask how I was feeling and *really*
listen to what I said. Susan was right. Deep down, I didn't believe I deserved it. And if I didn't, I was certain Mark didn't
either, which is why I kept attacking him!"

Once Patrice lowered her defenses with her friend, she was
able to express her desires to Mark. Doing so felt risky, but
wonderful. "I hated carrying on all the time about my needs not
getting met. It made me feel like the heavy in our relationship,"
she says. "Saying what I really wanted was frightening, it made
me feel incredibly vulnerable, but it broke the stalemate between us."

Mark didn't change overnight; at first he misinterpreted
Patrice's requests to mean she didn't want to be sexual, period.
Gradually he started touching her, holding her hand or putting
his arm around her, not necessarily as a sexual move, but as a
way to express feelings of warmth and attraction. Although he
wasn't an especially verbal person, he tried talking more and

paying more attention to Patrice's feelings. But it was Patrice's willingness to ask for what she wanted—*without* expecting and *without* blaming—that got them started on the right track together. When Mark responded with the willingness to try, their marriage couldn't help but get better. What Patrice did was both simple and enormously difficult. She began the process of letting go of her expectations, replacing them with tangible requests that she expressed in a direct, vulnerable way.

Why is this so hard to do? Besides extensive cultural conditioning, what are the reasons we persist in clinging to romantic fantasies when holding on to them is self-defeating? Why do we resist transforming unrealistic expectations into loving negotiations? As we will see in Chapter Five, at least part of the answer lies in the complex emotional baggage from the past that we carry with us into our relationships.

FIVE

BURIED TREASURE

Women ask: "Why can't I just decide to make this marriage better and then do it?" We want very badly for our relationship to live up to our dreams. What gets in our way?

The answer lies in understanding and coming to terms with the past. What happened then still matters now. To take down the wall and be more capable of intimacy in the present, we must do what we can to identify patterns of behavior and heal wounds left over from childhood.

The hard emotional work of excavating for buried treasure—uncovering unfinished business—enables us to see what *underlying agendas* we're acting out in our relationships with our mates. Unearthing this information—what it meant then and how it's affecting us now—frees us to take the reins in our lives, instead of being driven by ghosts of issues gone by.

Insight into the past is a necessary relationship tool. Without it, we just keep making the same mistakes.

Emily's Story

Emily, thirty-two, describes how hard she tries to be a better partner—and better person—in her marriage.

"I'm driving home and thinking about the fight Carl and I had last night. I have this whole thing worked out about how tonight I'm going to listen, I'm going to be patient. I'm *not* going to get into a screaming match. I even stop and pick up his favorite ice cream to have for dessert. Then I walk into the house and he's sitting there pouting because dinner isn't ready. He says sarcastically, 'Thanks a lot for coming home on time!' I throw the ice cream in the freezer, wondering why I'm still married to this jerk!"

After interviewing hundreds of women, I recognize this story as Emily's version of The Script. The specifics of women's scripts vary, but the basic scenario is the same: We want more. We try to do our best. We rehearse our moves ahead of time. Then he walks in, he looks at us the wrong way or says the wrong thing—and we move straight from disappointment to divorce court in our minds.

WHY IS LOVE SO MUCH WORK?

The intensity of Emily's feelings—and her hopelessness—are caused by the restimulation of old, painful feelings mixed up with present conflicts in her marriage. "Carl's always ragging on me," she explains. "He says he's on edge because he works so much, and he says he's sorry, but I think he apologizes just to shut me up. I'm not willing to give him a break anymore. The minute he blows it, I slam the door in his face."

Emily can't possibly know whether her marital problems are insurmountable until she separates what she's angry about in the present from what angered her in the past. How much of her rage is appropriately directed at Carl, who has disappointed her one too many times? How much is the leftover rage of a hurt and abandoned child? When we can't or don't separate the past from the present, the two merge in a confusing amalgamation. As Dr. Harville Hendrix explains in *Getting the Love You Want: A Guide for Couples,* "The past and the present live side by side in your mind."[1]

REVISITING THE PAST

It's natural to feel resistant at the thought of dealing with unfinished business. It may seem overwhelming to relive those memories, especially if doing so requires confronting our parents. Being hurt or not getting what we needed was bad enough back when it happened. Why put ourselves through it all over again?

Fortunately, we can do most of our healing work *without* involving the actual players from the past. Few families are sturdy enough to look honestly at unhealthy patterns or unresolved events; it's more common to disintegrate into blaming and shaming. *All* family members are threatened when one breaks the conspiracy of silence.

Is therapy the one and only way to go through this process? Absolutely not. Some people emerge from their families with relatively few scars. Others aren't comfortable with the idea of opening up to a stranger, regardless of whether that person is a trained professional.

If, for whatever reason, therapy isn't for you, a close friend or confidante may provide a sympathetic ear to talk over personal issues. A trusted member of the clergy can also be a valuable resource. For many people, support groups, workshops, or twelve-step recovery groups are safe places to share feelings, get feedback, and make important life changes.

Although there are different ways to process feelings, I believe that for many of us formal therapy or marriage counseling are the most productive choices. The first step is to find a skilled therapist who provides the right fit. The journey back to childhood can be bumpy, and is best traveled with an experienced guide to help ease the way.

Shopping for a Therapist

There are a number of ways to go about finding a therapist. Making a well-informed decision at a time when you are already upset can seem overwhelming. There are just two things you need to do: First, get the name of at least one qualified therapist. Then, briefly interview the therapist over the phone, and decide if you feel comfortable making an appointment.

Here are some avenues for finding a therapist:

1. A referral from a friend or relative is one of the best ways to proceed. If you know someone who's been in therapy, ask for their recommendation. Since therapy is a highly individualized relationship, you will want to get more than one referral if possible.

2. A member of the clergy where you worship.

3. Your local mental health clinic or family social service. (The United Way can direct you to either of these.)

4. Your medical doctor or the women's center at your hospital should have a list of therapists.

5. If you belong to an HMO, they will send you a list of therapists who are covered by your plan.

6. If you work for an organization with an Employee Assistance Program, you can obtain a confidential therapy referral.

In interviewing a therapist you will want to ask the following questions:

How would you describe the kind of therapy you practice?

What kinds of issues do you consider yourself most effective at dealing with?

On the average, how often do people come to see you? Once a week? More often?

How long do people usually stay in therapy with you?

What is your background and training?

What do you charge?

No matter what answers you are given in an informational interview, what ultimately counts is your gut feeling. If the

therapist seems warm and approachable, if he or she is someone you can imagine feeling safe with, that is more important
than all the degrees in the world. You needn't make any long-
term commitments. Try it out for a few weeks and see how you
feel. Remember, it takes time to build up trust.

Here are the names of three books that include additional
information on choosing a therapist:

How to Find a Good Psychotherapist: A Consumer Guide. Judi
Striano. Professional Press, California, 1987.

Getting The Love You Want: A Guide for Couples, "Seeking Professional Help" on page 274. Henry Holt & Co., Inc., 1988.

A Woman's Guide to Divorce and Decision Making, "Would
Counseling Help You?" on pages 30–31. Christina Robertson.
Fireside/Simon & Schuster, 1989.

"I wouldn't have known where to start," says Adrienne,
twenty-four, who admits she and her husband, Dennis, would
be divorced had they not gotten help. "Now," she says, "at least
we have a chance."

When Dennis told Adrienne he no longer felt attracted to
her, she decided to look for a couples' therapist. "I was scared
about going," she recalls. "I was afraid we wouldn't find anyone
we liked. And I was afraid I would discover something that
would cause our marriage to break up."

What Adrienne discovered was how many of her and Dennis's problems pointed back to patterns learned in their families. "We found out that lots of our disagreements with each
other were really about our family programming," she explains.
"For example, in both of our families, it wasn't okay to be angry
or to disagree, so whenever there was a conflict we either
avoided it or had a big fight over something little and stupid. We
were like puppets who were just acting out what we'd learned

in our families—mostly how *not* to be ourselves, which made it impossible to be intimate with each other."

After four months of weekly therapy sessions, Adrienne still isn't convinced their marriage is going to survive. At times she dreads going: "There are days when I just don't feel like exposing myself," she says, "but so far, it's worth it." She credits therapy with two significant breakthroughs: "We don't have big blowups anymore and some of the stuff we used to fight about doesn't seem so serious. We're down to a couple of core issues." The one thing she's still confused about is how to deal with her parents now that she's identified their part in creating patterns she's working so hard to undo.

Whether or not we seek formal therapy, it's important to realize that other family members may not want to look at their feelings and past issues just because we have decided to look at ours. Don't assume that timetables will coincide. People get there when they're ready, and there's no rushing it.

So how can we go about healing without confrontation? First, we must accept within ourselves that there's no such thing as a perfect family. Every family has its skeletons in the closet—whether Dad drank, Mom was depressed, big brother Mike failed his senior year of high school, or Aunt Ethel manipulated everyone in the family with her money. Every parent, no matter how loving, makes mistakes. We must first acknowledge, understand, and release the hurts we sustained when growing up in their care, then it may be possible to forgive them.

Allowing ourselves to reexperience the past—whether we do it by bringing up memories alone, with a friend, or with a therapist—takes courage and it takes time. Trust yourself to reveal only as much as you're ready to face.

GETTING THE GOOD STUFF BACK

One often overlooked benefit of doing family-of-origin work is the potential to embrace the wonderful experiences and positive messages we got. We assume we will be totally immersed in painful memories, but along with the pain reside feelings of pleasure and pride. As Melody Beattie writes in *Beyond Co-dependence and Getting Better All the Time,*

> We go back to the house we grew up in. We walk around to each dark room, turn on the lights, and look around. . . . We go back long enough to see what's happened and how it's affecting us now. We visit yesterday long enough to feel and be healed. We go to war with the messages, but we make peace with the people because we deserve to be free.[2]

Like many experts in this field, Beattie believes that the process of doing historic work involves grieving for what was lost during childhood. That grieving includes forgiving our parents *and* forgiving ourselves. True healing occurs when we reexperience childhood feelings, this time realizing we are not that same helpless child, but powerful adults who can make new healthy choices.

In *Toxic Parents,* author and therapist Dr. Susan Forward writes, "People need to get angry about what happened to them. They need to grieve over the fact that they never had the parental love they yearned for. They need to stop diminishing or discounting the damage that was done to them. Too often, 'forgive and forget' means pretend it didn't happen."[3]

Forgiveness, if it can be granted, provides a sense of relief and an opening to go forward with a greater measure of peace. Even if it's not possible to forgive now, the goal of exploring what happened during childhood is *not* to use what you discover as an excuse. I-got-hurt-so-how-can-I-be-expected-to-love-anyone is a way to avoid being responsible for your actions. What's important is to accept full responsibility for ourselves, here and now.

Remember: The point of unearthing buried treasure is to heal and be more fully present in our intimate relationships. There may be periods in this process of self-pity or great sadness. See them as stages, not as your final destination.

Personal Checkpoint

- What old, unfinished business from your childhood is getting in the way of your relationship?
- Are you willing to release and heal the past?
- What steps can you take to do so?

Strategy for Healing the Past

Tell yourself "I deserve to be free of past pain that's keeping me shortchanged."

Don't tell him "Being with you brings up terrible memories."

Do tell him "I am working to heal old pain. Please be patient with me."

The risk He won't be.

The reward You will be more able to give and receive love.

Doing historical work helps us to love him or leave him in these five ways:

1. We stop expecting him to make up for what we didn't get or what hasn't healed.
2. We address and resolve the real issues.
3. We react in proportion to what the situation warrants.
4. We stop repeating the same old patterns.
5. We are more capable of intimacy.

Let's look at each of these in turn.

1. *We stop expecting him to make up for what we didn't get or what hasn't healed.* Unmet needs from childhood combine with conditioned romantic illusions to create a whole layer of deep, sometimes desperate needs, and as we have seen, we project these needs onto our partner in the form of underlying agendas. For example, we may think that we expect our partners to provide financial support or companionship, when we *really* expect them to be mind readers, make us feel good about ourselves, and compensate for the deprivation we felt growing up. This amounts to filling a bottomless pit.

In *The Indispensable Woman* I use the term "payback kids" to describe the dynamic of wanting our children to provide us with the love, approval, and acceptance we didn't get when we were children. To an even greater degree, we expect our mates to "pay back" or compensate us for the losses or missing pieces in our past. We may even choose a mate based on this underlying agenda.

A woman whose father never touched her or told her she was pretty craves affection and compliments from her mate. Another woman who grew up feeling pretty but did poorly in school falls in love with and marries a well-respected professor who treats her as his equal. Another, divorced less than a year after discovering her husband's affair, is determined to find a man who will promise *never* to look at another woman. Still another, fifth in a family of seven children, goes through life starved for attention. She bristles when her husband suggests they have another baby.

Jennifer, who has been in therapy with her live-in partner, Phil, for eight months, explains: "One minute we're fighting about who folds the laundry, and the next thing I know I'm in tears about why he never holds me or tells me he loves me. I get all insecure about whether he's really committed in our relationship, which brings up all the ways I've never felt good enough and lovable enough."

We forget that *it isn't up to him to make us feel lovable, valuable, or safe.* It isn't anybody's job to do that for another person.

Hannah, a warm, thirty-eight-year-old writer, describes how unhealed wounds from her past affected her relationship with Jason, her husband. "For years I was after him to be more sexual with me. I wanted sex all the time. When he didn't respond, I'd feel desperate and hollow. I'd pout or yell and scream about how he wasn't attracted to me."

Hannah knew she was in pain, but it wasn't until she met other women who shared the same problems that she was able to stop projecting her unmet needs onto Jason. "I went to a weekend workshop on sexuality for women," she explains, "and I got in touch with all this yearning from my childhood. I remember willing myself to stay up as late as I could, hoping, praying my mother would come in my room and tuck me in, but she never did.

"Seeing myself as a tiny little girl who had needed so much love from someone who just couldn't give it, made me so sad! I cried and cried. Over a number of months, I grieved for that little girl who was me, whose heart never got held. And I forgave my mother."

Confronting her pain from the past—in a safe environment—took enormous pressure off Hannah's relationship
with Jason. As she shared with him the truth of how hurt she had
been during childhood, the trust between them deepened. However, it's still hard for her to let go of her past images of herself.
"I'm working on believing that I'm okay, which I guess takes a
long time. And I'm learning to appreciate Jason, and not expect
him to fix what happened to me long before we ever met."

2. *We address and resolve the real issues.* Hannah was able to
get down to the real stuff—her deep need for emotional nourishment that got thwarted in childhood. More often, we *think* we're
dealing with what's really going on, when in fact we've put up a
smoke screen. We waste enormous amounts of time, energy, and
emotional wherewithal keeping the real issues buried.

A classic avoidance behavior is to engage in ritual fighting,
those recurring conflicts that engage our interest, pump up our
adrenaline, and ultimately lead nowhere. Ask any couple, and
they'll easily name the one or two fights they have on a regular
basis.

Ritual fighting is never about what it appears to be about.
For example, we *seem* to be fighting over who takes out the
garbage; in fact, we're having a serious power struggle, trying to
negotiate the terms of autonomy and equality in our relationship. Or we *seem* to be battling over whose turn it is to take care
of the children; in truth, we're fighting over whose needs are
going to get met.

As long as we're mixed up about why and whom we're
fighting, there's no way to reach a satisfactory resolution. We
may come up with a temporary compromise or solution, but we
can count on the same issue resurfacing again and again.

Leah's Story

"For years, Greg and I kept having the same fight. There would
be something deeply personal I'd want to share, some intense

experience I'd had that was life changing and (I believed) urgent for him to hear about if he really wanted to *know* me. I'd initiate a conversation, usually starting with, 'There's something I need to talk to you about . . .'

"Almost immediately I'd get this strange sense that he was slowly disappearing, as if I were flying in an airplane and watching the trees, cars, and people get smaller and more remote, until they resembled toy-size pieces from a child's board game. I'd start to panic, then become enraged. But instead of saying so, I'd slip on my therapist hat.

" 'What's going on?' I'd venture, in a concerned, yet slightly detached voice. 'Nothing,' was his stock answer, followed by silence. I'd counter with, 'I'm feeling sort of distant from you,' remembering to make an I-statement, being careful not to sound confrontational. After a long pause he'd mutter, in his best here-we-go-again voice, 'Do you really want to know what's going on? What's going on is that I'm feeling overwhelmed by your intensity.' This would be followed by a twenty-minute dissertation on how pressured he was feeling, interspersed with vague references to being smothered by his mother and sideways jokes about my belonging in the *Guinness Book of World Records* for having the most feelings of anyone on the planet.

"Grateful that at least he was talking, I'd refocus my energy on helping Greg delve into his feelings. Before long I'd start feeling ripped off. 'Wait a minute,' I'd ask myself, 'how did this happen? Here I was trying to share my feelings, he withdrew, and now we're absorbed in discussing how he can't respond to me because of *his* feelings!'

"To add insult to injury, once he'd unloaded his anxiety and we'd spent a lot of time processing his stuff, he'd feel great. Suddenly he was all ears, eager for me to pour out my heart. Too late! By then, that was the last thing I wanted, because I was too resentful. And so we'd go in circles, around and around again."

Getting at What's Really Going On

It took Leah and Greg a long time to figure out why they couldn't break free of this pattern. First, with the help of group therapy, they realized that each had basically good intentions. The trouble was, each was acting out of patterns deeply rooted in the past, patterns they weren't even aware of.

Here's what was really going on: Whenever Leah tried to engage Greg in a personal conversation, he'd instantly feel pressured. *He* thought he was responsible for solving her problems (an impossible task!) when *she* just wanted him to listen. His sense of being overwhelmed stemmed from a long history of feeling responsible for his mother—an insecure woman who had been badly neglected by her alcoholic husband. When Leah turned to Greg for support, his suppressed rage at having had to take care of his mother came out at his wife. She and his mother were all mixed up in his mind.

Leah's impulse to shut down and push Greg away when he didn't immediately respond as she wanted him to was also an old pattern, motivated by feelings of shame. As far back as she could remember, Leah's parents had given her negative messages about being so emotionally intense. "You're just too sensitive," was their repeated put-down.

When Leah shared her feelings with Greg, and he didn't seem interested, *she* heard "too sensitive." His rejection—no matter that it came out of his own emotional limitations—reopened old wounds, making her feel unloved and angry.

Leah and Greg broke through this old pattern with honesty and a few agreed-upon communication strategies. Once they understood why this interaction was so emotionally laden, they were able to approach the problem more productively. Leah practiced monitoring her own intensity, being careful not to bombard Greg with too much information at one time. She learned to back off and give him more room, instead of expecting an instant response to her feelings. Knowing how fragile she felt, Greg stopped making wisecracks about her sensitivity.

Each promised to try to let the other know what was going on inside. Greg learned to say, "Wait a minute, I'm feeling pressured. I need a minute to regroup." Leah learned to say when she was feeling ashamed. Once they could separate the past from the present, they no longer experienced each other as The Enemy, but rather as a human being, each trying to do his and her best. They felt more loving, more compassionate, more able to move forward in the relationship.

3. *We react in proportion to what the situation warrants.* How do you know whether an issue you are dealing with is the "real thing" or a cover for more complicated issues from the past? In Leah and Greg's case, repeatedly getting stuck in the same place was the tip-off that they were missing something important. Another clue was the sheer size and intensity of their emotions. *When underlying, unresolved issues are present, we generally respond with a bigger emotional reaction than the situation warrants.*

When Leah approached Greg to share something important, instead of feeling slightly put upon, he felt as if he were about to be swallowed alive. When he didn't respond as she wanted, instead of being merely disappointed, Leah felt total rage and despair. Her knee-jerk reaction was to "sever the interpersonal bridge," a common response to shame[4] which, in the moment, feels essential for survival.

Most things seemed bigger to us as children. Have you ever gone back and visited the home you grew up in? The rooms are probably far less spacious than you remembered, the ceilings not nearly so high, the street out front narrower and less formidable. Feelings work the same way. The emotional experiences of childhood assume gargantuan proportions, especially those that occasion joy, sadness, anger, or fear. Things that happen when we are little, powerless, and less able to make sense of our feelings *stay fixed* as giant-size, technicolor memories that still can overwhelm us with their power.

Charlotte Davis Kasl, author of *Women, Sex and Addiction,* recommends taking a "temperature reading" when interactions produce intense reactions. When feelings register as "hot," there may be more going on than meets the eye. For example, when you're in the middle of an argument with your mate and you experience actual physical symptoms—your blood pressure rises, your throat closes up, you flash hot or cold or feel nauseated—there's a good chance you've hit on feelings from the past that you'd be wise to examine. If your mate says something that makes you feel so violent, so out of control that your impulse is to pitch a sharp object his way or walk out the door for good, then it's time to stop, call a time-out, and ask yourself these questions:

1. What am I feeling?
2. When have I felt this way before?
3. What do I need right now?

Connecting present feelings to the past provides a road map to the source of your emotions. If you can trace your feelings back to their origins—"I felt sad like this when I was eleven and my grandmother died and no one told me what was going on" or "This incredible rage reminds me of being six or seven years old when I was sick and my parents left me with a nanny and went on a vacation"—then you can begin to release, heal, and finally close the door on your leftover feelings from childhood.

But answering the first two questions alone won't alleviate the difficulty you're having in the present. That's where the third question comes in: "What do I need right now?"

Mara's Story

Mara, an actress married seven years, often feels more like a four-year-old than a forty-year-old when it comes to dealing with her husband, Sam. A black-haired beauty given to wearing exotic, colorful gypsylike clothing, Mara grew up on what she calls "the other side of the tracks" in Chicago. "We were poor kids and we knew it. I was always awed by those rich, white-bread kids I met at the Catholic church we went to—you know, the ones with scrubbed faces and starchy, Marshall Fields clothes. I never felt as good as they were."

The feeling of never being "as good as" other people followed Mara into her adult life, popping up unexpectedly whenever she felt insecure. And it influenced her choice of a mate. "When I met Sam, the first thing I thought of was, 'He's like those white-bread kids, not like the poor, dirty, ethnic kids on my block.' "

Mara was drawn to Sam's genteel, middle-class, and somewhat bland demeanor. He embodied respectability, which for Mara was the ultimate symbol of security. "He never raises his voice," she said, "and his socks are in perfect, neat rows in his middle drawer."

But Sam's blandness also needled her. She wondered how someone so even-tempered and orderly could be attracted to someone as passionate and volatile as she was. Deep down she saw Sam as superior to her, and whenever they weren't getting along she reverted to long-established, intensely disturbing feelings of being on the outside.

"We were at a party for Sam's firm at his boss's house," she recalls, "and I was in the middle of telling a story when I realized I was being very loud and gesturing dramatically. I looked around and all the other people there, especially the women, looked so elegant and discreet. All at once my voice seemed too loud and my purple jumpsuit that I've always loved seemed gaudy to me.

"I felt incredibly self-conscious and looked over at Sam for reassurance, but he was having a quiet conversation with his boss's wife, who looks like she came over on the *Mayflower*. Suddenly I wanted to escape. I wanted to kill Sam for abandoning me, even though we're usually pretty independent at parties and there was no reason he shouldn't have been talking to someone else. But I wanted to go, and I wanted to go right that minute! Sam agreed to leave. When we got in the car, I started in with him, accusing him of being ashamed of me. I backed him into a corner until he finally admitted that occasionally he wished I would 'tone it down.' And then I started crying because I was sure he didn't love me and would eventually leave me."

Once she calmed down, Mara asked herself the three questions: What am I feeling? When have I felt this way before? What do I need right now? She came up with these revealing answers:

1. *What am I feeling?* "I'm feeling scared and ashamed."
2. *When have I felt this way before?* "I felt like this when I was a little girl and didn't think I belonged."
3. *What do I need right now?* "What I need right now is reassurance."

Now Mara was ready to take care of herself in the present. After taking a deep breath and a big leap of faith, she asked Sam to tell her why he loved her and why he had married her. Her courage paid off in spades. Sam told her how much he appreciated her passion and flair, her rich exoticism and yes, even her emotional outbursts.

This opened the door for Mara to start building more confidence about their marriage, and more acceptance of the differences between her and Sam. With his support and the help of a therapist, she learned to release her past feelings of alienation, which enabled her to more fully embrace herself—purple jumpsuit and all.

4. *We stop repeating the same old patterns.* Had Mara never confronted her feelings of inferiority, she and Sam would have kept repeating scenes like the one at the party. In fact, by marrying Sam, she may have unconsciously chosen someone with

whom she could recreate her childhood situation so as to have the opportunity to work it out.

Many contemporary psychologists maintain that the unconscious drive to reconstruct patterns of the past is the primary motivator in our choice of an intimate partner. This comes, in part, from our pull toward what feels familiar. We instinctively return to unfinished business hoping finally to put it to rest. In Mara's case, that meant entering a relationship in which she could continue to see herself as conspicuously outside the mainstream, always the outrageous, insecure waif, always fighting to belong.

Robin's Story

"I feel like I'm fighting for my life," Robin says, describing the tumult in her on-again, off-again marriage of five years. In reality, she's been fighting a lot longer than that.

"My mother was very sweet, but very weak," Robin explains. "She was a typically passive woman of her era. She always gave in to my father. He was the gorilla in the family, always screaming and yelling."

An only child, Robin took on the role of her mother's protector and defender. "When I was six or seven years old, I'd hear him screaming at her down in the living room," she recalls. "Mother would run to her room crying and slam the door. Then I'd come down and finish the fight for her."

Robin was intimidated by her father's wrath; her knees would knock together beneath her thin, cotton nightgown. But she was driven by rage and a deep survival instinct: "I needed my mother, and I was terrified she'd go away if I didn't stop him from hurting her." Her empathy for her mother was so complete that she took on the job of parenting her.

Instead of feeling safe and cared for, she was, in effect, an orphan, streetwise within the intricate twists and turns of her family's emotional geography, with no way to relax and be the little girl she really was. How could her mother protect her when she couldn't protect herself? Her father was a menace, someone to avoid or fight with, who seemed capable of destroying them both.

And so Robin saw no choice. She mustered all her bravado and confronted "the gorilla" directly. Still, she was no match for him, and their screaming battles always ended in his severely punishing her. "But at least I fought back," she says, "and to this day I'm determined never to let anyone treat me the way he treated her."

The echoes of Robin's war with her father are evident in her marriage. Unknowingly, she married a man very similar to him. Aaron is loud, bullheaded, and temperamental, sometimes to the point of violence. Their relationship now provides the battleground on which Robin continues the symbolic fight. "I won't let him win, no matter what," she admits. "I'm out for blood over the littlest things. I can feel my adrenaline pumping and I start to hate Aaron. In that moment I want him gone, bloody, dead."

But Aaron isn't the enemy. At this point, neither is her father. She *can't* magically erase her painful feelings leftover from childhood. Her loss occurred a long time ago, and no matter how many times she reenacts the battle, her grievance is with her own, unresolved feelings, and that's where the healing must occur.

Robin *can* replay the drama within her marriage, only this time transforming the outcome. For example, she can learn to fight without wanting to kill. She can learn to protect herself while staying in the game.

5. *We are more capable of intimacy.* Facing our unresolved feelings from childhood increases our capacity for intimacy. "An intimate relationship is one in which neither party silences, sacrifices, or betrays the self and each party expresses strengths and vulnerability, weakness and competence in a balanced

way," says Dr. Harriet Goldhor Lerner in *The Dance of Intimacy.*[5] A tall order, from what I can tell.

The roles and rules present in our family of origin helped create a false self of sorts, a self that we carry with us into adulthood, reducing our confidence and ability to express our authentic selves. We are defined and limited by the role we are given by our parents. Whether it's "I'm the pretty one" or "I'm the smart one" or "I'm the one who keeps the peace," these rigid roles imprison us, preventing us from being fully and wholly who we are. Recovering our true selves—the real buried treasure—is what makes intimacy possible.

Jan's Story

"You know the saying 'The apple doesn't fall far from the tree'?" says Jan, a professor at a midwestern college. "It's taken years for me to stop behaving like a carbon copy of my mother!"

After four children, years of therapy, and so much personal growth that she barely resembles the eager-to-please nineteen-year-old bride she once was, Jan is able to look back on the family conditioning that gave rise to her patterns of behavior.

"My mother stayed home with us, and I just assumed that she and my father had as good a marriage as most people," Jan begins. "She raised us, kept the house nice, and pretty much saw it as her job to keep Dad's life in working order.

"But I knew Mom was unhappy. She was depressed a lot of the time, and she drank. She was a really good artist, but instead of pursuing her own career, she stopped painting when she married my father. She always resented him for it.

"My father would come home and Mom would be half in the bag. But no one on the outside knew. To the rest of the world we looked like the perfect family. We had money, we went to the right schools, and no one ever saw what really went on. The worst part was that you never knew when things would get crazy. The good times were great, but even then you were waiting for the other shoe to drop."

As the oldest child and only girl in the family, Jan learned early on to be a "good girl" and caretaker. "I always tried to do whatever I thought my parents wanted," she recalls. "I never rebelled because I was trying so hard to keep the family together."

But once she left home, the bottom fell out. Jan started skipping classes and fell madly in love with Hank, a law student two years older than she, whom she describes as intensely moody and charismatic.

"I gave him absolutely everything," she says. "My virginity, my identity. He decided who I was. We had a really hot and heavy sex life, but when I wasn't in his arms, he took perverse pleasure in being mean to me. Once when we weren't getting along I asked him, 'What's wrong with us?' and he answered: 'You're not pretty or smart enough.' I believed him." Having an affair with Hank's best friend, Mitch, was Jan's way of finally getting out of the relationship.

Then Jan met Terry, on the rebound. "I married Terry so I could cross the street," she says wryly, with a laugh. "My parents liked him. He was from a similar background, was working for his father's lumber business, and was a friend of my brother's. By marrying him I killed two birds with one stone—getting my parents' approval and moving out of their reach."

Once Jan and Terry married, she fell right into the role she'd learned so well in her family. "We were a perfect pair," says Jan, ruefully. "I automatically took over everything in our marriage. Terry was the youngest of four sons and his mother's favorite. He was spoiled and used to being waited on and getting his way. We fit together like a key in a lock."

Although she worked hard at having a positive attitude, forebodings of disaster crept in early in their relationship. "The night before our wedding, I had a nightmare that I was walking down the aisle with a faceless groom." Within days of returning from their honeymoon in Europe, Jan began to experience disturbing doubts and gnawing feelings of anxiety.

"I can remember sitting cross-legged on the couch facing Terry, trembling but forcing the words out, 'We need to talk.' I told him I felt all alone in our marriage. He looked at me as if I were nuts. I wanted something from him—friendship, emotional closeness, the feeling of being soulmates—but it was like getting blood from a stone."

So Jan threw herself into having children and searching for meaning in her own life. "With each child I became more involved with the kids and less available to Terry," she says. "I never stopped wanting to have a really intimate marriage, but, because we couldn't get anywhere, I tried finding answers myself. I became a vegetarian, I learned how to meditate, I kept a journal faithfully. I read every book about psychology I could get my hands on so I would keep growing as a person. I went to therapy, and although I couldn't get Terry to go—he doesn't like to talk about his feelings with strangers—I just kept going myself, hoping to find some peace."

For all intents and purposes, Jan operated as a single parent, almost singlehandedly caring for and disciplining the children, while keeping an immaculate house, volunteering for dozens of organizations, running two miles each morning, and continuing her journey toward self-knowledge. She became increasingly controlling, especially when it came to making decisions about the children. None of this bothered Terry. He was very traditional. He saw his role as breadwinner and provided a good living. He loved his work and had a regular foursome he played golf with. He wanted Jan to support him in his career—which she did—and take over with the kids. But he couldn't understand her unhappiness, why she had withdrawn sexually, or what caused her to lash out at him so often over little things.

When anyone, especially her close friends, asked about her marriage, Jan defended Terry, talking about how hard he worked and insisting she didn't mind the inequality in their relationship. But she was lying. Inside, Jan agonized, secretly questioning what she was really getting from Terry, and whether it was worth it anymore.

"I felt schizophrenic," she explains. "I'd meet people who treated me as if I were a nice, interesting person, and then I'd go home and be with Terry, who saw me as this cold, unapproachable bitch." Any emotional nourishment she got came from her children and from the stimulating people she met at the meditation center and at graduate school, where she had enrolled in the education program.

Jan's path brought her closer to herself but pulled her farther away from Terry. Without meaning to, she became increasingly bitter about how much work she was doing in the relationship and how few of her expectations were being met. Her marriage had become token—a source of financial security, but sorely lacking in emotional, spiritual, or sexual connection. She began to contemplate divorce, not because she really wanted out, but because she couldn't see a way to make her marriage better.

Jan and Terry definitely needed help. However, Jan was so fixed in her role of caretaker (read: martyr) that when problems arose, she automatically fell into familiar behavior—trying to control Terry, rather than negotiating for what she needed.

Because Jan had never known what it was like to be a child in a safe, protected environment, she didn't know how to be "little" or nurtured. As an adult child of an alcoholic, her only experience was in taking charge and coping—no matter what. Having never developed a sound belief in her own personal worth, she wasn't able to shatter her false self and stop taking care of everyone else at her own expense. She couldn't show Terry how badly she hurt inside or ask for the love she so desperately needed.

It took a separation and near divorce for Jan to see how unhappy she really was, as much with herself as with Terry.

Once she realized the extent of her addictive need to control Terry by taking care of things for him, she began to experience deep sadness at having had to be such a grown-up, even as a child. For several months she raged inside at her mother for being an alcoholic, but mostly for having thrown away her own life. Eventually Jan came to view her mother's condition as an illness, and she began to understand how her entire family had paid dearly.

As Jan saw her family with greater clarity, especially her own role as caretaker, she was able to look at the part she had played in creating rigid roles and greater distance between herself and Terry. She spent time with her mother, whom she had taken great pains to avoid in the past. Being around her mother was, in many ways, like looking in a mirror. They even spoke with the same inflections. When she nagged at Terry, she sounded exactly like her mother nagging Jan's father. She even pursed her lips the way her mother did when she was mad.

Testing the waters a little bit at a time, Jan and Terry experimented with changing the roles and rules in their relationship. She stopped making excuses for him and started including him more in her search for spirituality. She took up golf. He agreed to be home on time for dinner at least twice a week, and to spend more time with their children. She became warmer and more spontaneous; less like a drill sargeant, more like a lover.

None of this is easy. None of it happens just by wanting it to happen or without a great deal of emotional stamina. Like stripping away romantic illusions, healing our hurts opens the heart for true intimacy, so that we can safely reveal our real selves. Only by going back is it possible to go forward.

As we clear out the debris of childhood hurts, needs that never got met, and roles that have limited our own vision of ourselves, we can look at our mate right now, in the present, and ask ourselves, "Who is this person and what is *our* history together?" As we will see in Chapter Six, the wear and tear, strains, passages, and crises we weather in our relationships deeply affect the quality of love between us, testing our commitment over the long haul.

TIPS FOR HEALING UNFINISHED BUSINESS FROM THE PAST

- Recall a time from your childhood when you were hurt, scared, or didn't feel safe. Write it down as if it were a story or share it with a trusted friend. When you've finished, ask the child in the story (yourself) what you need in order to feel better.

- Find a photograph of yourself as a small child. Describe how you appear to be feeling. Notice any feelings of protectiveness or compassion you feel toward the child in the photograph.

- Ask a sibling to compare notes on your childhoods. See how your experiences compare and contrast. Share honestly what life was like growing up in your family.

- With the help of a professional, initiate a conversation with your parents about specific hurts that are lingering from the past. Be sure your goal is to heal and improve your relationship in the present, not to extract your pound of flesh.

- Try to remember all the wonderful, happy things that were also a part of your childhood. Make a list of all your best memories with each of your family members.

- Think about your finest qualities and characteristics. See whether you can trace some positive inheritances to your parents. If possible, share this information with them.

UNDERCURRENTS AND
TIDAL WAVES

I didn't realize how angry I still was until I came across a letter from that woman Paul had the affair with," Ellyn confided
over a coffee break with Pat, her office mate. "I was looking for
these bell-bottoms for a sixties party when I stumbled on it in
his drawer. Reading it made me sick! 'My dearest Paul, I'll never
forget what these past weeks have meant....' I wanted to
burn it."

"That's awful," Pat commiserated. "Are you going to leave
him?"

"Of course not," replied Ellyn. "Why should I ruin *my* life
over something he did eight years ago?"

It may have happened eight years ago, but it still hurts. No
matter how successful a relationship is, there will always be
some amount of pain, disappointment, or tragedy. No two people can live together without occasionally stepping on each
other's toes, and in some cases, colliding hard enough to cause
serious harm.

Some couples, like Ellyn and Paul, are hit by tidal
waves—major traumas that cause long-term damage and up-
heaval. Others are faced with constant undercurrents of
frustration; minor aggravations or chronic unresolved issues
that keep them from feeling satisfied and secure. Still others
encounter serious flaws or live with uncomfortable secrets

locked deep inside that make true intimacy impossible. In most relationships, little things, more like ripples than waves—the constant criticism, the hurtful remark made in a moment of anger—create static and diminish the quality of love between us.

Each relationship is unique. Each has weathered its own storms. But turbulence does not mean your relationship is doomed. On the contrary: Making it through hard times together can be transformative, strengthening the bond between you.

This phenomenon—of love deepened through shared experience, both good and bad—is apparent in some couples who've grown old together. When I look at photographs of my Papa Phillip and Grandma Sophie, their intense feelings of devotion and love, forged over fifty years of sharing joy and facing adversity, are evident in their eyes. If pictures could talk, theirs would say, "For better or for worse, we're in this together, and there's no place we'd rather be."

Papa Phillip and Grandma Sophie met with plenty of hardship in their lives, yet their love prevailed. Perhaps it's because they never expected marriage to be easy. Or maybe it's because they agreed, early on, never to go to bed angry. Just before Gary and I married, Grandma Sophie took me aside and whispered, "Be sure to get a bed small enough so that neither of you can hide. That way," she went on, "if you're having a fight, one of you turns over and gives a nudge, the other gives a little push, and before you know it . . ."

Grandma Sophie wasn't sophisticated, but she knew something important: Very few things are worth staying mad about. She knew, and I'm learning, that hard times can be either obstacles or opportunities, depending on how we deal with them. But when mistakes and transgressions are ignored or stuffed away instead of being aired and forgiven, the wall between us just grows more formidable.

Why Borrow Trouble?

The thought of going back over problems "hanging" in your relationship may seem as scintillating a prospect as your annual Pap smear. Perhaps less so, if you're not sure what you would gain. It's natural to want to avoid dredging up the past. After all, it was hard enough at the time! Who needs a replay?

But something happens when we don't come to terms with the past. These experiences leave lasting imprints. They inform our interactions with our mate and prevent us from appreciating the positive in the present. By exposing them, we begin to rob them of their power.

Time Warp

When we look at him, we don't just see who he is *right now*. He's not just Jerry, but Jerry-who-never-shows-up-on-time-for-dinner or Peter-who-takes-me-for-granted or Andrew-who-wouldn't-stand-up-to-my-father.

Every time he disappoints us, our confidence in having chosen the right person is shaken. Being a good father has always been his strong suit, then suddenly he leaves his four-year-old at home alone for twenty minutes while he runs to the post office. Or we've always thought of him as extremely stable, then he gambles away half the tax return money on the lottery, making us wonder, Who is this guy, anyway? Are these temporary lapses in judgment or serious character flaws? We're not sure if it's wise to forgive and forget.

Whether we wallow in them, cherish them, or push them out of sight, holding on to hurt feelings isn't the same as dealing with them. It stings to face them, and it scares us. Rather than honestly confront our anger and forgive our mate, we rationalize, saying, "Bringing it up won't help anyway, so I may as well forget it." Only *we don't forget*. These feelings remain unresolved, left to smolder and make surprise appearances in the midst of seemingly unrelated arguments, like uninvited guests at a dinner party. Old feelings announce themselves, suddenly dropping in to make trouble. And sometimes it's just when we think everything is going along well.

It's as if two disparate realities were functioning simultaneously. We may appear to be getting along famously, then, he says something innocent like "New sweater, honey?" and the next minute we're furious again over the red cardigan "guilt sweater" he gave us after betraying a pact years ago not to tell anyone we were pregnant. Or he reaches to embrace us and there's something about the way he brushes our cheek that brings back memories of a time we made love, when he made that insensitive "love handles" comment.

Some old hurts are easier to forgive than others. You may finally be able to let go of the Awful Thing that he's already apologized for a hundred times or learn to truly accept some chronic aggravations. Other issues take longer. It's a positive first step simply to let yourself know how upset you still are over something truly painful that needs more time to heal. In every case, being honest about what's happened in the past between yourself and your mate is the first step toward having a better relationship *right now*.

Rating Your Relationship History

How do you rate your relationship history? Would you say that, over the years, your relationship has been marked more by joyous experiences or painful disappointments? If you were to plot your relationship on a graph, would there be more peaks or valleys? Would a current photograph of the two of you reveal more embitterment or more intimacy?

Looking closely at our relationship history is worthwhile for many reasons. It gives us the chance to heal old wounds and celebrate forgotten joys. *But we must do both;* we can't just choose to focus on the good times. If we repress difficult memories or obsessively rehash them, the whole picture gets skewed and nothing gets better. Our relationship history includes a panorama of experiences—both positive and negative—that help make us who we are, both as individuals and as a couple.

The eighteen questions that follow are designed to help you start thinking about your own relationship history. Later in this chapter we'll use this information as a tool in letting go of old hurts. For now, simply try to focus on unresolved feelings that continue to affect how you feel and act toward your mate.

RELATIONSHIP HISTORY QUESTIONNAIRE

Section One

1. The little thing he does that really gets on my nerves is _____
_____.

2. I've asked him a thousand times to stop _____
_____.

3. I know he can't stand the way I _____
_____.

4. What disappoints me most about him is _____
_____.

5. We never stop arguing about _____.

Section Two

1. It really shocked me when he _____
_____.

2. The worst thing so far that's happened between us was _____
_____.

3. I haven't forgiven him for _____
   _____.

4. He's never forgiven me for _____
   _____.

5. One secret I've kept from him is _____
   _____.

6. He doesn't know that I know that _____
   _____.

7. I've had trouble trusting him ever since _____
   _____.

Section Three

1. The one thing about us I'm most proud of is _____
   _____.

2. I've been pleasantly surprised by how he _____
   _____.

3. The nicest thing he's done was when _____
   _____.

4. He really came through for me when _____
   _____.

5. I know I can count on him to _____
   _____.

6. I'm very grateful for his _____
   _____.

Your answers should reveal many of the undercurrents *and* tidal waves in your relationship. You may discover that you're having trouble getting beyond one, terribly hurtful incident from the past, or that a number of relatively small, but recurring issues keep getting in your way. You may have identified some of the obstacles and opportunities in your relationship and redis-covered some "forgotten" positive feelings toward your mate.

Depending on how comfortable your relationship is, and

how well you and your mate communicate (this means both talking *and* listening), you may want to use your completed questionnaire as a starting point for discussing your relationship history. Perhaps you'll want to give him a copy of the questionnaire to fill in, then see how your answers compare. PROCEED WITH CAUTION! The questionnaire is meant as an exploratory device, *not* as a weapon for hurting, accusing, getting back, or getting even. You may prefer to raise these issues only with the support of a professional counselor.

However you choose to make use of the information gained from the questionnaire, it should now be easier to identify which of the following six issues are present in your relationship:

- The Little Things that Bug you.
- Reruns.
- Secrets.
- The Terrible Thing he said (or did) that you never Forgave or Forgot.
- Bombshells.
- Life crises.

Let's consider them one at a time.

1. *The Little Things that Bug you.* He leaves the toilet seat up, the convertible top down. When he brushes his teeth, he scatters thousands of tiny spit marks on the mirror. His clothes stay where he drops them. He says dinner was great, but disappears before the dishes are washed. He calls to say he's running late, forty-five minutes after the fact. And you'd faint dead away if it ever occurred to him to find a baby-sitter.

Okay, so he's not perfect! What woman can't produce an extended list of Little Things that bother her? And if you asked him, he could undoubtedly do the same.

Living in close quarters gives us a microscopic view of him in a way that both illuminates his best features and magnifies his most annoying character traits. Unfortunately, it's natural to focus on what we don't like. His bad habits get on our nerves; his strengths we tend to take for granted. It's like going out on a lovely summer day, then spending the better part of it being irritated by a fly buzzing around your face. What's bothersome earns your attention; what's pleasant goes without saying.

As we settle in, there isn't as much romance and excitement to balance our irritation over Little Things. Our anger that nothing has changed—when we've asked and asked and asked—builds up over time, hardening into resentment.

How much we notice and are bothered by the Little Things is an important litmus test of how we are doing in the relationship. When we're upset with or feeling estranged from our mate, irritants that might otherwise go unnoticed or unremarked upon suddenly have the power to drive us crazy.

The Little Things don't cause horrible fights or divorce in and of themselves. Have you ever heard of anyone standing up in divorce court and saying, "Your Honor, I left Larry because he parked the car so close to the middle that there wasn't room for my car in the garage"? Probably not. It's when we're *already angry* that the Little Things become too much to ignore.

Strategies for Living with the Little Things

CHOOSE YOUR BATTLES

It's safe to say that the Little Things won't just go away, not without some real efforts at communication and commitment to change. This is one area where you're wise to choose your battles—to decide what's worth getting upset about and what should be left alone. Strategically, it's important to decide what things bother you most and how much of a problem each one really is. This exercise can help.

STEP 1: Make a list of all the Little Things that irritate you.

STEP 2: Go down the list and ask yourself the following three questions about each item:

1. (a) Does it annoy me only slightly or (b) is it something that makes me want to tear my hair out?

2. (a) Does it irk me occasionally or (b) do I think about it several times a day?

3. When I think about my mate (a) is this irritant relatively meaningless or (b) does it immediately spring to mind, coloring my perceptions and feelings?

For every "b" response give yourself one point, for every "a" response zero points.

STEP 3: Divide your original list into four separate lists: three-pointers, two-pointers, one-pointers, and zero-pointers, according to your scoring from Step 2.

STEP 4: Finally, look at each list and circle the items you think your mate is capable of changing. Be realistic!

Now you've got something you can work with—a list of Little Things you *know* bother *you* and you *believe* your mate can do something about. Using this list, you can choose your battles and stop trying to fight the whole war at once.

For example, asking him to start picking his socks up off the floor—even if he seems constitutionally incapable of doing so, even if he offers dozens of reasons why he can't—*is* reasonable, and it's something he most likely can achieve. On the other hand, he may not be able to do anything about his shyness, snoring, or other more deeply ingrained problems. Even though these things may also grate on your nerves, it's best to make up your mind to learn to live with them.

F I G H T O N E at a T I M E

It's overwhelming to deal with a never-ending list of complaints. If you inundate your mate with all the Little Things at once, you can make him feel as if he is under attack and hopeless to change any *one* thing.

Tackling one Little Thing at a time improves your chances of success. Start with the one he's least defensive about and most willing to deal with—that way he'll feel less threatened about the ones that follow.

Be sure to create some breathing space in between. No matter how many Little Things are on your list, bombarding your mate with one after another will backfire. Both of you need time to recover from battle fatigue. Victories over the Little Things should be celebrated with a gentle, noncombative period of appreciation.

D O N ' T S E C O N D - G U E S S H I M

One caveat here: Learning to live with the Little Things that bug you can be an excuse to avoid dealing with them. Too often we don't give our mate enough credit. We assume that he can't or won't attend to our concerns, when in fact he can and he may if we give him half a chance.

Resist the urge to second-guess him. Doing so can result in a self-fulfilling prophecy. For example, you want him to stop making "fat" jokes; you're sure that nothing you do will convince him to stop, so you don't ask. By anticipating his response, you send him the message that you are resigned to being on the receiving end of his jokes, which, of course, he keeps making. This reinforces your belief that he won't change, bringing you full circle.

D O N ' T C O M P L A I N a b o u t H I M t o O T H E R P E O P L E

Along the same lines, resist the urge to grumble or complain to other people about your mate. Bending a friend's ear (or worse, your child's) about deficiencies in your mate is only another way of avoiding dealing with them. It constitutes a betrayal of your mate's feelings and confidence. No matter how much you try to give a fair account, you can't help but subtly turn others against him. And, although complaining may give you temporary relief, in the end, it undercuts your confidence in the relationship. The more you tell the wrong person, the worse you feel about the person you should be telling. Try approaching him directly and respectfully; you'll get better results.

BE CAREFUL ABOUT HOW YOU APPROACH HIM

Of course, bringing the Little Things out into the open doesn't mean they will magically improve. He may say yes; he may say no. He may get angry and start reeling off his own list of grievances. When confronted, people tend to become defensive and dig in their heels. Habits *are* hard to break—as you know, if you've ever tried to break one yourself.

It helps if you're careful about *how* you approach him. If you come on too strong, he might resist just *because* you're asking—stubbornly refusing to accommodate before he's ready. When this happens, a Little Thing becomes the basis for a full-fledged, down-and-dirty power struggle.

"I'll be damned if I'll stop playing poker with the guys on Thursday nights just because Lynn doesn't like it!" says her husband, Jack, defiantly. "She knew when we got married that I was independent, and it didn't bother her then. But now she's always on my case. If she wanted someone who'd sit home every night, holding her hand while she watches television, she should have married someone else!"

When we become locked in a power struggle over a relatively unimportant issue, it's almost certain that something bigger is lurking beneath. His refusal to be civil to your father may really be about his own feelings of insecurity concerning where he fits into your life. Maybe your unwillingness to thank him when he does you a favor reflects ongoing resentment that he doesn't help out much with the day-to-day chores. These chronic issues require a more concentrated look, perhaps with the help of counseling.

Trying to win a power struggle is futile and exhausting. The *real* issues are elusive and bound to reappear under another guise.

D O N ' T   T A K E   I T   P E R S O N A L L Y

Learning to detach from your mate's flaws and foibles is imperative if you don't want to keep beating your head against a wall. It can be useful to repeat to yourself, "This isn't about me," when he's doing something that annoys you. "Someday, should I be lucky enough to live that long, he may remember to close his closet door before leaving for work," said one wife of ten years. *But*, the fact that he doesn't is no reflection of his love for her.

Like many women, I take things personally. I'm quick to say, "If he really cared about me, he'd . . ." rather than realizing his habits are just . . . habits. They say no more about his feelings for me than my failure to clean out my car says anything about my commitment to our marriage.

Bottom line: How much we let the Little Things bug us is really up to us. We can let them rule our feelings or go about changing those that are changeable and let go of the rest.

2. *Reruns.* You might think of reruns—chronic issues—as the *big* things that bug you, only they never stop. Chronic issues vary greatly from couple to couple. One woman grapples with her husband's workaholism while another complains that her spouse can't hold down a job. Another woman is plagued by in-law problems, another has blended-family complications, while others cope with chronic money difficulties, poor communication, or sexual incompatibility. Chronic issues slowly eat away trust and confidence in your relationship. It's demoralizing to keep working on the same old stuff, especially when nothing seems to get better.

Ruth's Story

"I wasn't prepared for Tom's workaholism," says Ruth, a freelance decorator and mother of three-year-old twins. "When we were dating he studied hard and was ambitious, but I didn't expect he'd work sixty-five hours a week and never see the kids."

After trying nearly everything—sympathy (effective only short term), elaborate scheduling, marital counseling, ultimatums—Ruth was at her wits' end. She felt lonely and victimized. When she spoke of Tom, her comments were laced with sarcasm; she still loved him, but her marriage, particularly the way he handled fatherhood, just wasn't what she'd bargained for. When they fought about Tom's never being home, he'd say, "If you need help, hire help." She'd say, "The girls need their father, not another baby-sitter." He'd say, "I need time to run my business!" She'd say, "Pretty soon you'll have more time than you know what to do with!" And on and on it would go, deteriorating until both took refuge in stony silence.

Ruth and Tom were at a standstill until a year ago, when their world was cataclysmically turned upside down. Janie, one of the twins, came down with a life-threatening illness. She spent a month hospitalized, with Ruth at her side. Tom was forced to cut back his schedule in order to care for their other daughter. Suddenly Tom found plenty of time to reflect and reassess his priorities. Having nearly lost his child, and possibly his marriage, he vowed to set limits at work and devote more time to his family.

While a dramatic event like Janie's illness can push chronic issues into the forefront, precipitating sweeping changes, lasting change usually comes slowly—in fits and starts—and necessitates taking the long view. One year later Tom has done a fairly good job at keeping his bargain, but not without further talk, planning, and compromise on both sides.

"Tom and I constantly negotiate and renegotiate who's going to do what and when," Ruth reports. "He's gotten a lot better about the kids, but I've accepted that I have to keep pushing him so he won't backslide."

Lowering our expectations because we're convinced that chronic issues won't change no matter what we do, is a defeatist attitude. What doesn't get better gets worse.

Identifying Chronic Issues

You may have chronic issues in your relationship if . . .

- You keep having the same fight over and over.
- Some subjects of conversation are taboo.
- The same issue has been present in your relationship for longer than six months.
- In thinking about a certain issue, you feel like giving up.

Suggestions for Coping with Chronic Issues

Counseling and therapy are good ways to approach chronic issues, because most are deeply rooted in dysfunctional family patterns. Understanding where they come from helps us detach and be more empathetic toward our mate.

But what if he just isn't willing to do anything about them? Worse yet, what if just bringing them up enrages him? If he's not ready to change, there's no way to rush him. It's up to you to decide whether, for now, you can let go and live with chronic issues, without making yourself crazy. Meanwhile you'll have to take care of yourself by setting some boundaries. Yvonne learned to do this in coping with her husband's chronic lateness.

"I couldn't count on Rafael ever to be anywhere on time," recalls Yvonne. "I was always on him about it, but it never changed. I was constantly embarrassed, calling friends to say we were late again. I can't tell you how many times dinner was spoiled while I waited for him to come home. When he finally showed up, I'd be angry and end up looking like the heavy."

Yvonne finally got so frustrated that she went to a support group to talk about her feelings. "I learned that I couldn't control Rafael's lateness, but I *could* set some boundaries. I went home and laid out my new rules: that if he was more than fifteen minutes late, I'd pick up the baby-sitter and go to the party myself. That the kids and I would start dinner without him if he wasn't home within twenty minutes of our agreed upon timetable. I reiterated that this was my way of taking care of myself, not an attempt to punish him."

After numerous cold dinners, Rafael got the message that Yvonne was serious, and he started working harder at being on time. It's still a problem, but Yvonne no longer feels angry and victimized.

Bottom line: If chronic issues are severely affecting your quality of life, it's time to take action.

PERSONAL CHECKPOINT

- Go back to section one of your Relationship History Questionnaire on pages 140–141 and list any chronic issues you see.

- Which of these are you willing to accept, let go of, or work on changing?

- What would it take for you to accept, let go of, or work on changing the rest?

- How can *you* make this process easier for yourself?

3. *Secrets.* Should you or shouldn't you? Tell, that is. Every relationship has its secrets. Little secrets, like you've always

hated his favorite orange shirt with the bluebirds on it. And big ones, like the fact that twelve years ago his older brother put the moves on you and you've never breathed a word of it.

Secrets are inherently dangerous because they put distance between you and your mate. Hidden over a long period of time, secrets take on a life of their own. They preoccupy us and assume a certain amount of drama and importance. Our secrets become infused with precious energy that could and should be used more productively.

Most women keep a certain amount of "necessary secrets" from their partner, choosing not to divulge information that's either too personal, none of his business, or potentially damaging to the relationship. When Jackie spent a wonderful afternoon reminiscing with her high-school sweetheart after running into him at their twenty-year reunion, she wisely chose not to tell her husband. "I knew we wouldn't see each other again," she explains, "and telling Ted would only have angered him or made him feel insecure."

There's no rule that says we have to share everything with him, and in fact we shouldn't. Deciding which secrets to tell and which not to tell is a highly individual judgment call. In a hilarious scene from the movie *When Harry Met Sally . . .* , Sally (Meg Ryan) convinces a naive Harry (Billy Crystal) that all women, at one time or another, fake orgasms. She demonstrates her technique in a crowded luncheonette, panting and squirming in full voice, and we come to believe that this is one secret—probably universal among women—better kept than shared.

How do you know which secrets to share and which to keep? Three *trouble signs* tell you if secrets are getting in the way.

A PATTERN OF PRETENDING. Pretending is one way of keeping a secret: You act one way even though you feel another. Often women pretend in order to avoid conflict or because it seems easier than being honest about their feelings. When women pretend to be happy, pretend to be satisfied, and pretend to be content while secretly harboring resentment, they are headed for trouble.

FREQUENCY. Whether we're borrowing from the household budget to buy clothes for ourselves or the kids, getting together with old boyfriends, or keeping something else under wraps, frequency is a second indicator of trouble. *How often* we keep the same secret tells us if we're keeping the lid on a problem that should instead be brought into the open.

CONSISTENCY. Consistently behaving in a secretive way spells trouble because it engenders mistrust. Keeping an occasional secret is very different from leading a secret life. For example, he probably doesn't need to know that when the two of you made love last night, you were mentally writing out your grocery list. But if you've been faking it four out of five times for the past year or so, it's *past* time to talk about it. The two of you need help with your sexual relationship, and you're not going to get it as long as you continue to pretend.

Situational Ethics

If you should decide to tell your mate a secret, it matters *why* and *when* you tell. Secrets can be used as weapons when exposed at the crucial moment. *Think* before letting him know that he bored everyone to tears at the alumni dinner with his dumb jokes and endless anecdotes. If he asks for your input, fine, but there's a way to give feedback without being brutal. Blurting out hurtful comments, even in the so-called interests of honesty, is a low blow and damages trust.

If there are secrets standing between you and your mate, ask yourself *why* you are keeping them. Are you afraid of getting into an argument? Do you believe your relationship is too fragile to survive the release of such classified information? Are you punishing him or keeping him at bay by withholding important information in order to protect yourself from feeling vulnerable?

Letting secrets out takes away their power to cause strain and tension in your relationship. Keeping secrets can be a way of keeping him out. What he knows about, he can do something about.

Bottom line: Don't keep secrets that harm the intimacy and trust between you and your mate.

4. *The Terrible Thing he said (or did) that you never Forgave or Forgot.* "We promised each other we wouldn't tell anyone we were engaged. It was our secret. Three days later his best friend congratulated me."

"We were having dinner with his whole family and his sister started a big argument with me. Pretty soon his older brother chimed in. Then his mother and his father. He just sat there silently."

"After twelve hours of labor, in the middle of a really horrible contraction I grabbed his arm and he recoiled. It was only for an instant, but I've never forgotten how abandoned I felt."

"Howard and I were out at a restaurant and Sid, an exlover of mine during college, turned up at the next table. He was warm, as was I, and Howard just flipped! We got into a horrible argument and he actually called me a filthy slut! I've never forgiven him."

These are isolated incidents, each the unforgettable result of bad timing, poor judgment, or angry feelings vented in a destructive way. When they happen, we wish we could turn back time, but there's no going back.

When a Terrible Thing is left to fester, it gets more terrible with time. It stays strong, painful, and current, permanently polluting our feelings toward our mate.

Once a Terrible Thing happens, its effects are hard to erase. We wonder: If he was so callous before, how do I know he won't be again? Or: After being so hurt, how can I possibly trust him anymore? He may insist that he never meant what he said or did, but deep down we don't believe him. He may even apologize, but that doesn't feel like enough.

Love Means *Always* Having to Say You're Sorry

In 1970, the movie *Love Story* attracted record audiences, leaving an indelible, romantic impression on the throbbing hearts of millions of teenagers, including yours truly. In the movie, then-ingenue Ali MacGraw and co-star Ryan O'Neal make up after an awful fight with the now immortal line: "Love means never having to say you're sorry."

It has taken me years to stop believing that if you *really* love someone there's no need to make amends. What a crock! Now I know that if any two words are necessary to the long-term survival of an intimate relationship, those words are "I'm sorry."

Often, saying them doesn't seem like enough. We may shrug off our partner's apology—even when it's utterly sincere—because it seems too easy. Or because it doesn't really change anything. But it's a start, and without it, there's no way to begin the process of forgiveness.

However, it's critical to note that the words *I'm sorry* only make a difference if they're accompanied by true remorse and the desire to make amends. Here it's useful to make a distinction between "guilt" and "guilty fear."[1] The first consists of an individual acknowledging blame and making an honest effort to examine and correct his mistakes: "I did it. I'm sorry. What can I do to make it up to you?" Guilty fear, on the other hand, is how we typically react to getting caught. It goes something like: "Uh-oh. I'd better do whatever I can to get off the hot seat, either by saying the 'right' words or diffusing the tension." When we're willing to express guilt, closure is possible. We can confront difficult issues, forgive and go on. But with guilty fear, the effort to run away leaves a continuing fear that nothing will change, which is why women continually batter away at the same issues, never feeling confident of resolution.

The good news is: When we deal with a situation *immediately*, it's easier to forgive and forget. If we can't forget, a formal apology at least makes it easier to function day to day without constantly reliving our painful memories. After all, everyone makes mistakes. The trick is to acknowledge them, express honestly how we feel about them, and get busy rebuilding trust.

Some women are angry and bitter over one particular incident; for others, bad moments have added up over time, creating cumulative tension and mistrust. If there's something he said or did which continues to haunt you, then *it's worth bringing up,* no matter how much time has elapsed. Here is a way to begin the healing process: Close your eyes, picture your mate, and imagine yourself walking toward him with open hands and an open heart. If anything gets in the way—a memory of a hurtful incident or a comment that still stings—then that's where you should focus your attention; that's where you should start.

Of course, your mate may also be holding on to something *you* said or did that *he* hasn't forgiven or forgotten. Collecting transgressions and competing for the Who's-Been-Most-Hurt Award is a bleak and unsatisfying basis for romance and intimacy. It's a no-win proposition that serves one and only one purpose: to keep the two of you safely at arms' length. It's much more productive to try to get beyond the past! Doing so is a delicate proposition, which requires patience, goodwill, and considerable finesse.

Strategies for Forgiving and Forgetting the Terrible Things

Some therapists recommend that couples use what I call a Forgiveness Ritual, in which partners take turns bringing up hurtful memories in a nonblaming way. Here is an example of a basic forgiveness ritual you can try with your mate, if he is willing; a cooperative partner is essential to success. (If you're working with a therapist or counselor, you may want to ask him or her to lead this exercise for you.)

F O R G I V E N E S S   R I T U A L

STEP 1. Person A makes a simple, declarative statement like, "I felt hurt when you forgot my thirtieth birthday" or "I was angry when it took you two hours to come to the hospital after Billy fell out of the tree." Avoid accusatory statements like "You hurt me . . ." or "You made me angry when . . ."

STEP 2. Person B responds with a statement acknowledging and affirming Person A's feelings. For example: "I hear that you were hurt when I forgot your thirtieth birthday" or "I know you were angry over how long I took to get to the hospital."

Person B is not expected to defend himself, nor is he required to apologize. However, if that person honestly *feels* like apologizing—if an apology is sincerely forthcoming and deserved—it is entirely appropriate at this point to add, "I'm sorry that you were hurt or angry." Then switch roles.

And that's all there is to it. Easy! The beauty of the Forgiveness Ritual is that neither partner is put in the uncomfortable position of having to provide long, involved explanations (which really don't matter) or of trying to make up for what's happened (which really isn't possible). The exercise omits blame. Instead, each partner is free to empathize with the other person's hurt and acknowledge that it happened, regardless of the reason. Each is free to say, "I realize you were hurt and as someone who loves you, I care about that."

Often it's simply enough to be heard—to know that our feelings are taken seriously, that our mate understands us and cares enough to listen and respond. This in itself can help soften old, petrified feelings of anger. If we're on the other end—if we're the one hearing about the hurt—it's a relief to be calmly told instead of attacked. This enables us to transcend our individual pain and relate to our mate's hurt in a way that enhances feelings of compassion.

More Strategies for Finding Forgiveness

As an alternative to the Forgiveness Ritual, you can try something similar called the Naming Ritual. All it involves is naming and "putting" your hurts into a garbage bag, literally and figuratively, one by one, then disposing of them. The symbolism of acknowledging and discarding old hurts together can be very healing. This ritual usually works best after couples have spent some time in counseling and feel sufficient goodwill toward each other to reinvest in their relationship.

Coping with Resistance

What if your mate nixes both approaches to releasing old hurts and finding forgiveness? You can still decide to help *yourself* through this vital process.

Some women write a letter in which they express all their feelings, uncensored, to their mate. Some mail their letters; for others, it's enough just to get the feelings out. Some women join support groups or enter counseling or therapy. Still others— and this I recommend for everyone—make a concerted effort to count their blessings, remind themselves of all the wonderful things about the man in their life, and put their disappointments in perspective. Whatever you choose to do will be an investment in the best interests of your relationship and in your own peace of mind.

What if you can't or won't let go of the past? This may be a sign that it's too soon. Give yourself some leeway and try again later. Then, if you're still unable to forgive him, you might ask yourself, "What would it take?" If there's any way he can make amends, let him know. Give *him* a chance to try.

The person who won't forgive, forget, or think about letting go of the past is usually getting something out of hanging on to the hurt. Often we trade feelings of self-righteousness—and the control that comes with it—for intimacy. By staying hurt, we hold all the cards. This is a hollow victory. When it comes to long-term relationships, being right is no substitute for being loved.

Bottom line: Sooner or later, it's necessary to heal and forgive the Terrible Things in order to safely take down the wall.

PERSONAL CHECKPOINT

• Go back to section two of your Relationship History Questionnaire on pages 140–141. Note any Terrible Things you have listed.

• Are there any you would be willing to forgive and forget?

• If not, why not?

• Is there anything *he* can do to make amends? What?

• What can *you* do to put these issues to rest?

5. *Bombshells.* Sometimes something happens that's so painful we don't think we'll ever get over it. A major betrayal—discovering that our mate is having an affair, finding out that he's addicted to alcohol or other drugs, learning that he has lied to us in a big way—can shake our trust to its very foundations.

Kate's Story
Kate knew about Matt's bisexuality when she married him, but at the time, he insisted his involvements with men were a thing of the past. It wasn't until two years into their marriage—when she was eight months pregnant with their first child—that he dropped the bomb.

"I had just come from my ob appointment to meet Matt at our favorite Mexican restaurant," Kate recalls. "He seemed agitated and I asked what was going on. He said he'd run into this guy he'd traveled with years ago in Europe. 'I don't know how to say this,' he ventured nervously, 'but I was incredibly attracted to Stuart. I just can't deny my feelings about men.' Matt confessed that he'd lied to me, that he hadn't gotten men out of his system after all and that he thought about being with them all the time. In the same breath, he promised me he hadn't slept with anyone since we'd been together and that he didn't intend to start. I tried not to get hysterical. All I could think about was being a single mother."

The subject got sidetracked in Kate and Matt's excitement over their baby's birth, and its importance receded even more as Matt proved to be a devoted father. But it was far from the end of it. Over the next six years, there were more explosions, usually without warning.

"Once, in the middle of a fight, Matt started screaming about how he couldn't truly love me as long as I didn't acknowledge his bisexuality. Another time we were out to dinner with friends, and he casually mentioned that there was this whole side of himself he had to repress. No one picked up on it, but I knew what he was getting at," says Kate.

"That night we went home and I told him I was sick of being the policeman in our relationship . . . that I wasn't willing to be responsible one more day for keeping him from being who he is. I told him if he needed to sleep with men there was nothing I could do to stop him, but that as far as I was concerned, our marriage would no longer be monogamous!" Shortly after that conversation, the AIDS crisis emerged, at which point Kate reconsidered her position. "Now we were talking life and death," she says. "I told Matt that it just wasn't worth it—if he decided to sleep with a man, he had to tell me, and from then on we would be friends, that's all."

Matt assured Kate that he was committed to their marriage

and wouldn't act on his desire for men. He said that it was no different than any heterosexual man choosing to be monogamous, but she wasn't convinced. "I knew I could compete with any woman, but a man? It was terrible knowing that there was some fundamental way I couldn't satisfy Matt, no matter how hard I tried."

For the next year the subject of Matt's bisexuality once more receded into the background of their careers, three children, and busy social life. Kate all but put it out of her mind, save for a few isolated incidents—once when she found men's magazines hidden under the bed and another time when a local video store called with a message that *Boys Will Be Boys* was overdue. Still, for the most part he seemed attracted to her and was, in fact, a sensitive and talented lover. She felt increasingly secure, until they went on vacation to the Bahamas and the bottom fell out.

"Matt had seemed preoccupied at the beach, but later we were watching the sun set and having a very romantic conversation. I asked him, 'What do you dream about?' And he burst out: 'You want to know what I dream about? I dream about *men!*' From that moment on it was vacation from hell. All we talked about for ten days was his bisexuality. It was awful, just awful. When we got home I told him to go figure out who he was and what he wanted and to quit tormenting me with it."

After years of denial, with occasional revelations, Matt's bombshell in the Bahamas finally forced the whole truth out in their marriage. Kate admitted to herself that Matt's bisexuality wasn't going away. She told him how vulnerable and scared she felt and how little trust remained, especially because his story changed every couple of years. She also told him that as long as he was committing to remain monogamous, she'd rather not hear about his bisexuality. She suggested he seek support elsewhere.

Matt joined a monthly support group of gay and bisexual

husbands and fathers where he could talk openly about his yearning for men *and* his choice to be married to Kate. Since then, he has stopped needing a secret life in order to affirm all sides of himself. Still, at times he finds it painful to be in a strictly heterosexual relationship: he wonders if he's in the wrong place, as does Kate.

"This isn't what I bargained for," she says, "and I'm still not sure I'm willing to live with the uncertainty of being married to a man who could run off with 'Raymond' any minute. But then, I guess there's no guarantee with anyone. And I always wonder if his wanting men keeps him from being as intimate and attracted to me as I would like. But for now, there's enough that's good between us to keep me here.

"I have to believe Matt when he says he's committed. Still, sometimes I look at him and I feel like I'm looking at someone I don't even know. With all his deception and wavering back and forth in the past, I can't help wondering what else he's been keeping from me."

When our trust is violated by our mate—the person we're supposed to be able to trust more than anyone in the world—we sustain a hurt so deep that we may not be able to imagine surviving intact. This is especially true in situations like Kate and Matt's, where what began as a bombshell has become a chronic issue. Once the dust settles, we are left with pain, fear, and a good deal of anxiety. Being let down by someone we love leaves us vulnerable and insecure. We may question everything we hold near and dear in the relationship, wondering whether we will ever be able truly to love again. And we worry and worry, looking over our shoulder, waiting to be hurt again.

"I'll never, *never* forgive Andy for the affair he had two years ago," says Shari, age thirty-five. "Although we just had our ninth anniversary, I can't forget what he did to me—the out-and-out lies! Sometimes it's worse than other times, like when we see a movie about someone sleeping with someone they shouldn't be or when I hear about someone whose husband is having an affair.

"I get paranoid if Andy is late or I don't know where he is. Last week he was supposed to be home from a meeting by eight fifteen, and at nine I still hadn't heard from him. I started pacing back and forth, getting more anxious as each minute passed. I was so nervous I even poured myself a drink. When he walked in at nine forty-five and apologized for having gotten tied up, I lit into him as if he'd committed a murder!"

When trust has been shattered, it's common to feel as if something—or someone—has died. If you have suffered a loss of this magnitude, it's important to allow yourself any and all of your feelings: sadness, rage, mistrust, grief, despair, and more. It's important to give yourself as much time as you need before trying to start rebuilding your relationship, if that's what you choose to do.

Although your partner, friends, or family may try to rush you, only you will know if and when you're ready to risk trusting again.

What About Him?

So far we've been assuming that your mate will be a willing partner in your efforts. But what if he isn't? What if he won't acknowledge your feelings, apologize, or even discuss the problem? Some men will continue to deflect responsibility, insisting that "it's her fault" and refusing to budge from this position. If this happens to you, consider waiting and approaching him at another time. Or agree to disagree. Or seek professional help for yourself.

You may hesitate to go to therapy or a support group alone because:

•   You may be afraid that doing so will anger your mate and provoke more conflict between you.

- You may be afraid that you will grow and change, leaving him behind.

- You may be afraid that facing problems will be overwhelmingly painful and lead to divorce.

- You don't know what to expect in the way of results.

All of these are reasonable fears. If your mate doesn't acknowledge the problems in your relationship, and/or is dead set against the idea of therapy, your going may make him feel threatened or angry. There's a good chance you *will* grow, as you gain personal insight, and that you will be less tolerant if he's unwilling to look at himself. And, it is possible that in honestly confronting your issues you will choose to end your relationship. These are *worst-case* scenarios; they are worth being realistic about, but shouldn't keep you from getting help for yourself.

The positive side is that going through therapy may profoundly enhance the quality of your life, both as an individual and as an intimate partner. As you develop greater self-awareness, your mate may become more interested in joining you in therapy or may find his own way of exploring his feelings. Identifying and facing your issues will help you to focus on problem solving and strengthen your commitment to your marriage, which is Paula's reason for seeking therapy.

"I haven't even told Tony that I'm going, because he'd go nuts," says Paula. "He doesn't believe in therapy. He says people who have to go hire someone to talk to must really be crazy."

Despite Tony's parochial attitudes, Paula has chosen to get help for herself. "Lately, I've been really unhappy," she says. "I've had trouble living with how conservative and closed-minded Tony is, especially in how he treats our children. He's much stricter than I am, and we seem to have very different values, even though in lots of ways I really love him."

Paula's secret plan is to go to therapy for six months, work hard at her goal of "learning to accept myself and accept Tony," and then tell him the truth, hoping he'll see how much happier she is and attribute the changes to therapy. It's a calculated risk, but one she's willing to take. "The whole plan may blow up in my face," she admits, "but at this point, I don't see what choice I really have. I need to do what I can do for *myself*. I'm just crossing my fingers that Tony will come around."

Tony may or may not come around, but in any case, Paula is taking important steps to feel better about herself and her relationship. Notice how clear her goals are: to accept herself and accept Tony—not change him.

A final reason we may hesitate to go into therapy is that we don't know what to expect in the way of results. Here are some common therapy goals, both for individuals and for couples, that may help you clarify whether this is the right tool for you in helping to heal relationship issues:

Therapy Goals

1. To identify the unresolved hurts, chronic issues, and bombshells that divide you.
2. To understand better the family patterns underlying your behavior—including why you've put up with unpleasant, even intolerable behavior from your mate.
3. To learn skills for improved communication and forgiveness.
4. To clarify the bottom lines of what you need and expect in your relationship.
5. To be more satisfied and fulfilled in your relationship.

After the Bombshell: Survivor Guidelines

As you are working your way through this difficult process, keep the following Survivor Guidelines in mind.

• *Know that you can survive.* Whether or not your relation-ship can survive the bombshell, *you* can. Even if it's time to rethink your commitment, *you* will be okay. You'll probably hurt a lot, and perhaps for a long time, but you *will* come out in one piece.

• *Be honest about your feelings.* Pretending that everything's all better or that your anger has dissipated isn't good for you, your mate, or the healing of your relationship. Honesty is the only possible starting point for healing what's happened.

• *Get help for yourself.* If you have been hurt by a bombshell, you owe it to yourself to get help and support. Be willing to let others—particularly those who have been through similar experiences—help you through this difficult time.

• *Realize that things are never going to be the same again.* There is no way you can erase what happened, and it's unlikely that you can pick up where you left off. However, change isn't necessarily bad or something to fear. Although it may not seem so at the time, it's possible that your relationship might even benefit from the bombshell.

• *Decide if you are willing to try again.* It's up to you to choose whether you are or aren't ready to try again. You have the right to do this on your own timetable. Will you give your relationship another chance or not? Making an active choice allows you to feel more powerful.

• *Make an active effort to trust again.* If you are willing to try, then work at reestablishing trust. Carol Botwin, in her book *Men Who Can't Be Faithful,* says that in the aftermath of an affair,

> it may not be easy, and it won't happen overnight, but it is possible [to trust] if you really want to. It isn't that he can't be trusted in all ways. You can learn to focus on the ways in which he can still be trusted. Think of all the ways he *can* be counted on every time you feel that you will never be able to trust him again.[2]

• *Go slowly*. There's no way to make the river flow faster; trying to will only muddy the waters. Trust that with time, you will be able to repair and recover.

Bottom line: Bombshells are serious betrayals that require time to heal. Surround yourself with love and support.

PERSONAL CHECKPOINT

• Go back to section two of your Relationship History Questionnaire (pages 140–141) and identify any bombshells you've listed.

• What scars have you sustained from these bombshells? How have they limited your trust?

• Which, if any, have you forgiven your mate for?

• What would it take for you to heal and forgive the others?

6. *Life Crises.* Like bombshells, life crises hit with the force of a hurricane, ripping apart a relationship and leaving a trail of damage in their wake. A death in the family, the loss of a job, serious financial trouble, or severe illness are typical life crises that couples face. Each one creates considerable turmoil, testing a relationship's strength and endurance.

The death of a child probably rates as the most devastating life crisis of all. The loss is so unimaginably painful that, at least in the beginning, each parent agonizes and grieves privately, finding it almost impossible to comfort the other. Following the loss of a child, it is natural to feel bitter; to curse ourselves, the world, and God; and to close our hearts and not let anyone in. It is not uncommon for partners to blame each other, desperately seeking reasons where there aren't any. Just being with him may make the loss more palpable, evoking painful memories of hopes and dreams.

Rita's Story

"At first I couldn't even look at Max without thinking about our son," says Rita, her eyes filling with tears. She shows me a framed photograph of their son, who died of leukemia at age seven. "Being with Max reminded me of every precious minute we spent together as a family. I hated him, and I hated anything that reminded me of my child. I couldn't bear to have any hope, to let myself imagine ever feeling happy again."

Rita and Max are among the fortunate ones. Over time they have healed together, finding strength in their shared experience.

"We gave each other a lot of space," Rita explains, "and we didn't expect much from each other for the first few years."

Adds Max, "There was a long period when I really didn't think we were going to make it. I couldn't break through Rita's shell, and I know I was miserable to live with; I guess neither of us could reach out. I buried myself in work and we kind of stopped talking to each other.

"Going to a grief support group was what really changed things for us," Max continues. "There were other couples there, in different stages, going through many of the same things, which helped a lot. But for me, the turning point came the night Rita broke down and talked about the morning our son died. I thought my heart would break. For the first time I really felt how much we had *both* lost, and how much we'd each suffered, all alone in our grief. We both wept. We held hands, and vowed to help each other through this. It's taken a long time, but having lived through this, I've seen how strong Rita really is, and how vulnerable, which has brought us much closer."

Darla's Story

Surviving a life crisis often requires a fundamental change in how we look at our partners. This is particularly true when a spouse becomes ill or unemployed.

"It's been seventeen months since Wayne got laid off, and the strain has been unbelievable," says Darla, thirty. She had just started graduate school when the firm her husband worked for restructured, laying off several employees.

"Right now I'm looking for a part-time job. Forget about graduate school. Meanwhile, Wayne mostly lies around the house being depressed. He's having trouble interviewing, although he's made a couple of halfhearted stabs at finding a job.

"I don't know what to do," Darla confesses. "I feel so ripped off. Even though I know getting laid off wasn't Wayne's fault—I know that he didn't do it *to me*—I resent having to quit school and help support us. I want to be there for him, but I worry about whether this will ever change. For now, I'm in a holding pattern."

Pulling Together

How Darla and Wayne come through their crisis depends, in large part, on whether they can put their individual feelings aside and pull together as a couple. Each has several hurdles to overcome.

Will Darla accept Wayne's dilemma, expanding her image of him from confident breadwinner to vulnerable human being who happens to be going through a particularly rough time? Will she be willing to shelve her career goals temporarily without becoming bitter and unhappy? Will Wayne find the inner strength and resiliency to rebuild his career? Will the two see Wayne's layoff as an opportunity to pool their resources and forge bonds? Or will they grow farther and farther apart?

Life crises, like bombshells, are often important turning points in relationships. How we respond to our mate in a time of trauma—whether we are supportive and loving, or allow our feelings of fear and anger to reign—can permanently alter the future of our relationship.

Bottom line: We *can* survive life crises if we are truly committed to honestly confronting our pain and supporting each other.

Getting support—and lots of it—is a critical part of this healing process. Depending on where you live, numerous and varied support groups exist, focusing on specific kinds of life crises. Sharing with other people who have had similar experiences can be enormously comforting. Some are peer support or 12-step recovery groups, for people coping with issues ranging from chemical dependency to codependency to living with cancer to getting through divorce. Short-term, professionally facilitated support groups are another option; your local hospital or mental health center is a good resource for finding the right group.

The undercurrents and tidal waves in your relationship may be caused primarily by past, unresolved problems, by stormy issues that continue to cause turbulence in the present, or by both. What's important is to identify what hasn't been healed and work on forgiveness.

Our ability to forgive our mate depends, in part, on what is good and positive about the relationship. Ultimately, the Little Things, Reruns, Secrets, Terrible Things, Bombshells, and how we survive Life Crises are weighed against the many ways we love, admire, and respect our mate.

R E I N V E S T I N G

It's impossible to shake hands with clenched fists," Indira Gandhi once said. She was talking about political peacemaking, but her words ring equally true for intimate relationships. As long as we approach our mates with clenched fists and closed hearts, the wall we've built between us stays firmly, painfully in place.

We have seen how the wall goes up. Now it's time to take an honest look at yours and decide—on balance—if it's worth taking down. Are you willing to open your hand and extend it toward your mate?

"But why should I make the first move?" you might ask. The answer is simple: because of what *you* stand to gain. The key to reinvesting in your relationship is to *do it for yourself.*

WHAT HAVE YOU GOT TO GAIN?

There are three things to gain from reinvesting: hope, happiness, and power. Just saying, "I'm willing to try" may seem like admitting defeat, but in fact, it's a statement of optimism. We must put aside our pride and self-righteousness in order to reinvest. We may feel as if we're giving in, but we're really giving ourselves and our relationships another chance.

Reinvesting increases our potential for happiness, but shakes up the status quo. We get so used to being lonely, hurt, and disappointed that feeling good seems strange and scary. Our comfort level is at risk simply because we're changing old patterns. We have to build up a tolerance for happiness and literally *learn* how to feel good again.

Finally, reinvesting gives us power. No matter how things turn out, taking action makes *us* feel better about *ourselves.* We may not get what we want. Our mate may not welcome the change. But we feel stronger, more alive and in control. Doing *something* is almost always better than doing nothing.

THE NEW WOMAN

A positive vision is pivotal to reinvesting. The ability to "see" ourselves as satisfied instead of shortchanged is essential to making it happen. When I speak to women on how to stop being "indispensable," I emphasize the importance of picturing what it would be like *not* to carry the weight of the world on their shoulders. The same holds true for finding happiness with our mates. Just as a builder needs a blueprint, we need a positive vision of ourselves to strive toward.

A positive vision describes how we would like to be in our relationships. It is a composite picture, one that inspires us to keep trying. It is *not* an unattainable ideal against which to measure ourselves.

PERSONAL CHECKPOINT

- What is *your* vision? Out loud, on paper, or to yourself, describe what it would be like to be your *best self* in your relationship? What changes would you make? What changes are you already working on?

IN OUR OWN BEST INTERESTS

A positive vision is the first step toward reinvesting. Self-love is the next step.

We have to love ourselves enough to believe we deserve the rewards inherent in taking down the wall. Our yearning is great. Deep down, unless our disappointment has brought us to a point of no return, we want to feel softer and more conciliatory toward our mates. Doing so means pushing through the frozen ground of our anger and hurt to the seeds of hope underneath. We hunger for connection, for the healing that will bring us closer together.

Ultimately, we reinvest for ourselves, because holding on to hurt and anger is nowhere near as nourishing as making peace with our mates. Staying stuck drains our energy. We become bitter, brittle, and unapproachable. We think we are punishing him when we are really hurting ourselves.

"How did you stop being furious at your husband?" I asked Catherine, who complained that he ignored her. "I got sick of myself!" she answered. "One day I was raging at James and I caught a glimpse of myself in the mirror. I looked awful! So unhappy! My lips were set in a miserable grimace, and I thought to myself, 'Wait a minute. Is this the kind of person I want to be?'"

The answer was no. Seeing herself consumed by anger inspired Catherine to make changes, starting with telling herself the following: *I am a good person in a good marriage that, like every marriage, has some problems. I don't have to let the problems destroy my happiness.*

"I decided to stop letting his behavior make me crazy," she says. "I concentrated on getting more attention from my friends and enjoying the things that I like about James."

Catherine didn't give up on trying to improve her marriage. On the contrary, her commitment grew as she focused on the positives.

Nothing changes until you *do* something. Waiting for him to move first usually results in a stalemate. As each side waits for the other to change, the situation deteriorates. Someone has to break the impasse for peacemaking to begin.

STRATEGY FOR REINVESTING

Tell yourself   "This relationship is worth working on."

Don't tell him   "When *you* start acting as if you love me, *I'll* get serious about our relationship."

Do tell him   "_____ is getting in the way of how I feel in our relationship. I'd like us to work on it together by _____."

The risk   He may be defensive or say, "There wasn't a problem until you brought it up."

The reward   Renewed optimism on both sides.

WHAT MEN SAY

What about the other side? Success naturally depends a lot on our mates. What do men say about their responsibilities to heal their relationships? Are they ready to make the kinds of changes we are asking for?

Like women, men have varying definitions of intimacy and differing visions of what would make them fulfilled. In general, I have found, men report fewer complaints and a higher satisfaction level with their mates. However, they commonly complain about being confronted by women's unmet needs. In my interviews with men of widely diverse backgrounds, I repeatedly heard them say of their wives, "I wish someone would tell

me just what it is she wants!" Some appeared genuinely confused and concerned. Others seemed resistant. A few were out-
right angry at what they perceived as women's unrealistic
demands.

Many expressed sincere commitments to doing "whatever
it takes" to improve their relationships. They consistently
shared visions that were so loving they gave me shivers. My
respect for men's seriousness about working on their relationships grew as I heard heartfelt comments like these:

> "I want us to look at each other at the end of each day and
> know that here is the one person I trust most in the whole
> world."

> "We need to respect that we're different. Then we could
> really love each other."

> "We're closest when we let each other see that we're just
> two flawed human beings, trying to get by."

> "I want us to walk side by side toward God."

If you're thinking, "That's nice, but you clearly didn't talk to
my husband," maybe it's time you took another look. Maybe you
can't see how hard he's trying, or hear how much he really
cares. Or maybe he isn't trying hard enough and never will.
Some men really *don't* care to make the necessary effort.

Whether he does or doesn't, reinvesting involves becoming
receptive to *any perceivable effort* on your mate's part. He may
be changing a lot, or maybe just a little, perhaps not enough to
make it worth your while to remain in the marriage. He may be
growing, but not in the particular way you want. You may withhold support for the progress he *is* making, for fear that you'll
give him the message that he needn't keep on his toes.

This idea is a myth. Acknowledging improvements is important both to you and to him. You need to see what's good in
order to know where you stand; he needs positive reinforce-

ment in order to keep trying. If you're unwilling to give credit where credit is due, it may be because of your own fear of taking down the wall.

FEAR: OUR BIGGEST OBSTACLE

Even with the best of intentions, change is difficult. Some mornings we wake up angry, unwilling to bend; other days we feel hopeful and optimistic. I wish it were possible to wave a magic wand and muster the guts and goodwill it takes to make a relationship better. But wishing is no substitute for accepting the adult challenge of rebuilding intimacy. Lasting change takes place in an atmosphere of faith and trust: faith that our efforts can be fruitful, and trust that whatever risks we take, we will still be all right.

We don't always have the wherewithal. What we have instead is *fear,* the four-letter word that destroys more relationship potential than anything else. Fear keeps us stuck. When we're afraid—afraid we won't get what we want, afraid we *will* get what we want and it won't be enough, or just afraid to try something new—we handicap ourselves and our relationships.

Lauren, thirty-five, describes her eight-year marriage as "stagnating." "Bob and I seem to have settled into a routine," she says. "Basically we have an okay marriage, it just isn't very passionate or stimulating like it was in the beginning." Lauren experiences free-floating disappointment, which she has a hard time pinning down to any particular problem. When pressed to explain what is missing in her marriage, she comes up with one chronic issue that has gradually eroded trust between herself and her husband. "There's this way Bob has of putting me down," she says. "It's subtle, but whenever I'm feeling good about something, he either makes a joke or in some way diminishes me."

Lauren is stuck. She can't imagine how to get beyond this issue and breathe life back into her marriage. But when I suggest that she confront Bob with her feelings and ask him to stop this behavior, she refuses. "Every marriage has problems," is her opening argument, followed by: "Why should I bother when he's the one who's doing something wrong? Anyway, bringing it up will only make him mad. Besides, Bob is Bob. Trying to change him is pointless."

Lauren's resistance is based on these five *fear-based beliefs* that help hold up the wall. Each reinforces a "do-nothing, gain-nothing" point of view that must be challenged in order for the wall to come down.

Fear-Based Belief #1: "It won't change anyway."

Challenge: How do you know unless you try?

Positive experience is the antidote to hopelessness.

Fear-Based Belief #2: "I'm too hurt or angry."

Challenge: Are you interested in healing or staying stuck?

Healing is the antidote to hurt.

Fear-Based Belief #3: "Let's see some results first!"

Challenge: What are you waiting for?

Action is the antidote to ambivalence.

Fear-Based Belief #4: "It takes too much energy to try."

Challenge: How much energy are you putting
                              into polishing your armor?

Motivation is the antidote to passivity.

Fear-Based Belief #5: "I don't want to rock the boat."

Challenge: Is your relationship worth taking a
                              risk?

Hope is the antidote to fear.

Allowing fear-based beliefs to dictate our behavior results
in paralysis rather than movement. Confronting these beliefs
means facing the fear and *choosing* not to let it reign. It means
adopting *confidence-based beliefs* instead.

Confidence-based beliefs help bring down the wall because
they are hopeful. Hope translates into action, and action leads to
change. Here are five confidence-based beliefs:

1. Change is possible.
2. It would feel good to let go of my hurt and anger.
3. I am capable of creating results.
4. Love and healing generate energy.
5. It's worthwhile to try *for my own sake.*

Let's see how replacing fear-based beliefs with confidence-
based beliefs makes a difference in Lauren's marriage. What
happens if she says to herself, "I'd really like to get over feeling
hurt and angry at Bob, so I'm going to tell him how I'm feeling
and what I want. Maybe if I explain how I'd like him to treat me
he'll be able to respond differently. In any case, it's worth a try!"

Lauren feels better—more energetic and hopeful—just
thinking about what she can do to get past this stumbling block
in her relationship. Her positive attitude motivates her to get
"unstuck."

Approach your relationship with hope and confidence, and you will be amazed at what's possible. Reinvesting yourself— heart and soul—is empowering. It's the first step toward being more fulfilled as a partner and as a person. As the poet Goethe wrote, "Whatever you can do, or dream you can, begin it. Boldness has genius, power, and magic in it."

Bold Moves

Taking down the wall requires a bold commitment to making two types of change: *Inner Shifts,* or changes in attitude and perception, and *Outer Moves,* or changes in behaviors and communication. Both are necessary to reinvesting.

An Inner Shift occurs when we alter our way of looking at something. An Inner Shift can be relatively ordinary, such as seeing the need for recycling when we used to toss newspapers without thinking twice. Or it may be profound, like confronting our own racism when our twenty-year-old daughter comes home from college with a boyfriend of a different color.

An Inner Shift can creep up gradually, so subtly we don't see it coming. Or it can come in the form of an epiphany: a sudden, dramatic awakening that takes us by surprise. Whether small or large, subtle or earthshaking, an Inner Shift means *we're seeing through new eyes.* We have changed, and as a result we act differently.

Sometimes an Inner Shift occurs as our perceptions or attitudes become outdated. Mary, a free-lance writer whose recent second marriage followed a nasty divorce and two tough years as a single mother, describes how she became aware of just such a shift.

"I stayed up late one night editing a manuscript. When I finally finished at two A.M. and went to bed, Joel was dead asleep, his entire body spread over my side of the bed. My knee-jerk reaction was anger at him for taking up my space. I felt invaded.

"But then I looked at him, his arms wrapped around my

pillow, and I could see that he missed me. Suddenly his being on my side seemed sweet! Right then I realized I didn't need to be so self-protective anymore. That I could get rid of my old picture of constantly having to protect my territory."

Elizabeth, a high-school teacher, found that an *outer* change in behavior was followed by an *inner* attitude shift. "I was in an awful place about David," she explains. "I didn't trust him, and I didn't really believe he loved me, or at least he didn't act as if he did. He was cold and he hardly ever confided in me, even though we'd been married five years. I'd about given up."

Elizabeth's unconscious response had been to mirror David's behavior. Normally warm and outgoing, she too had become distant. She had stopped sharing her feelings and initiating conversations, secretly hoping he would notice and do something. When he didn't, she decided that extreme measures were in order.

"What I had been doing obviously wasn't helping," she says, "so I decided to try the opposite. For one month I conducted a 'scientific experiment': I tried being nice. No matter how David acted, I was warm toward him. Basically, I treated him the way I wanted him to treat me, just to see what would happen."

Her experiment got results. "David *did* become more responsive, but what mostly changed was how I felt inside. Being nice to him made me *like* him more. I found myself really wanting our marriage to make it."

Some experts argue that Inner Shifts must occur before behavioral changes can stick. Others are convinced that if you change the behavior, new attitudes naturally follow.

In fact, it doesn't really matter which comes first. Deep Inner Shifts support Outer Moves and enhance their long-term success. It's also true that changing behavior—especially when we experience positive results—makes us feel and think differently. When Elizabeth acted more loving toward David, she found she felt more loving too.

In the remaining chapters, we will focus on three Inner

Shifts—and their accompanying Outer Moves—that are guaranteed to improve your relationship. If you're willing, they will move you . . .

> . . . from *ambivalence* to *commitment*
> . . . from *self-victimization* to *empowerment*
> . . . from *adversaries* to *allies*

Each shift involves a movement from one attitude to another, which is best envisioned as taking place on a continuum. Somewhere along each continuum is a moment of truth when we turn the corner from feeling shortchanged to taking charge of getting what we need.

EIGHT

FROM AMBIVALENCE TO COMMITMENT

There's no guarantee that getting off the fence will improve your relationship, so hedging your bet naturally seems like a safer position. But there is no way to know what's possible unless and until you put *all* of yourself *all the way* into your relationship.

Making the shift from ambivalence to commitment—getting off the fence—means that you:

- STOP making excuses.
- STOP waiting for him to make the first move.
- STOP settling for less than what you want.

Moving toward commitment means that you suspend your cynicism and act as if your relationship were worthy of the best love and energy you've got—even if you aren't entirely convinced.

Sound scary? Premature? Out of the question? Of course it does. But when we hold off from committing, waiting for proof that our mates will respond the way we want, we keep shortchanging ourselves.

Gail, thirty-two, and her husband, Arthur, thirty-seven, have been at a standoff for months on the subject of babies. He wants one. She does too, but she won't give him the satisfaction until she gets more of what *she* wants in their marriage.

"Having a baby means making a huge commitment to each other," says Gail, "and I just don't see us doing that until we're on more solid ground. My own parents divorced when I was six. I wouldn't want my child to go through that."

Gail paints a fairly gloomy picture of her marriage, yet she and Arthur appear reasonably happy together. Their marital issues are typical: fights over whose family to visit at Christmas, over money, over handling all the stress in their lives, especially since Arthur started graduate school. Having a baby *will* add pressure to their relationship, but it will also add joy.

"Until I'm absolutely sure that our marriage will last, I don't want to bring a new person into it," she says. "There's something about being a family that's different from being a couple. It's sacred. And it's forever."

Gail keeps waiting for Arthur to prove his love before she's willing to take the next step with him. Her ambivalence keeps her from jumping all the way into their relationship. At least once a week, she and Arthur have a heated argument that goes something like this:

Arthur: "Have you thought any more about having a baby?"

Gail: "I asked you to stop pressuring me."

Arthur: "I'm not pressuring you. I just don't see what you're waiting for."

Gail: "I don't know. I guess I just don't feel totally secure that our marriage can survive all the demands of a baby."

Arthur: "What do you want? A guarantee?"

Gail is afraid of making a mistake if she *does* commit (a genuine risk, but one worth taking), and in some ways she's more comfortable with her ambivalence. She's not totally ready to give it up.

She doesn't have to. The shift from ambivalence to commitment isn't an all-or-nothing proposition. At the moment Gail and Arthur are polarized, but what happens when each moves a short distance from their position?

Arthur: "I'd like to talk about where each of us is right now about the baby. Is that okay?"

(Arthur opens by acknowledging that they may not be in the same place and respectfully asks Gail if she's willing to talk about it.)

Gail: "I feel pressured just thinking about this subject, but I'll try."

(Gail owns her feelings of pressure instead of blaming them on Arthur. She makes a preliminary commitment to participate in the conversation.)

Arthur: "I can understand how you feel pressured. I feel worried that time is passing and we're not making a decision about this."

(Arthur affirms Gail's feelings. Instead of criticizing her, he acknowledges that he's worried about their extended impasse.)

Gail: "I'm worried too, but mostly about how much having a baby will change and put added stress on our
marriage. I guess I need more time to be ready."

*(Gail accepts Arthur's fears and shares some of her
own. She resists making dramatic, sweeping statements about their marriage "surviving" "all the
demands" of a baby, and asks for more time, which is
the most optimistic sign Arthur's had after months of
gridlock.)*

In this softer, more loving exchange, Gail and Arthur each
express their honest feelings, but without blame or defensiveness. They each move out of their polarized positions and together, agree to a plan: For the next six months Gail will
seriously examine the roots of her ambivalence, and they will
concentrate on areas of their relationship that need strengthening. During this time Arthur will back off and not pressure Gail.
If, after six months, they're still at a standoff, they'll seek professional counseling to help them resolve their conflict.

Even after counseling, Gail may not feel fully confident and
committed. It's perfectly okay to have reservations, to waffle
back and forth between feeling "this will never work" and "we
were meant to be together." The latter attitude comes most frequently in bursts—singular moments when we're flooded with
positive feelings that inspire us to want to be fully "in" our relationships. These bursts occur either when something happens
to remind us of how much we love and value our mates, or when
we're especially tuned in to what's really important in our lives.

"I have experienced both," says Louise, a wonderfully wise
thirty-eight-year-old therapist. "There are days when I'm feeling skeptical or halfhearted about my marriage, when Bruce
feels like a stranger. But then I catch a glimpse of him and my
son, Teddy, curled up together on the couch, our little boy's

head resting on his father's shoulder. Suddenly I am overcome by love, appreciation, and an inner conviction of rightness about our relationship.

"Other times, a burst of inspiration occurs when I'm alone, sitting by the lake or writing quietly in my journal. When I'm reflective, I get in touch with my gratitude and with a deep sense of meaning and purpose. At that moment, everything seems simple. Feelings of anger and bitterness fall away in light of the bigger picture. I resolve to be nicer, more accepting, and more compassionate. I understand that Bruce and I are together for a reason: to bring out the best in each other as true life partners. Right here. Right now. Today."

STRATEGY FOR REDUCING AMBIVALENCE

Tell yourself   "My ambivalence is really my fear."

Don't tell him   "This will never work. I don't know why I put up with it."

Do tell him   "I'm afraid of not having _____ in our relationship. Can we work on this together?"

The risk   He will use his knowledge of what you're afraid of to hurt you or to prove that it's your fault that your relationship has problems.

The reward   A stronger commitment toward your mate.

Living Your Real Life

We may shy away from making commitments because they require us to act *now,* in the present, without procrastination. "Life isn't a dress rehearsal," reads one of my favorite bumper stickers.

Yet many people go through life as if it is, holding out for the "real thing" instead of investing fully. A man constantly fantasizes about his dream wife instead of loving the one he has. Or plods along doing mediocre work, sure he is meant to be a deep sea diver, not a postal clerk.

But, for better or worse, this *is* your real life. This *is* your real mate *and* your real relationship. You won't wake up tomorrow to discover someone else lying next to you. And besides, that's not really what you want. What you want is more love, intimacy, and fulfillment with the real man in your life *right now.*

There are dozens of ways to rationalize our lack of commitment. "These are the tough years," one woman says, sounding burdened and exhausted as she explains why she can't possibly hire a baby-sitter so she and her husband can have a few uninterrupted hours together. What she means is: "Right now I'm too overwhelmed by all the pressures in my life to make time for my mate." Similarly, women say "When the children are grown . . ." or "When my work schedule slows down . . . ," their voices trailing off into the distance, expressing the shortsighted belief that their intimate relationships can wait five, ten, or even twenty years without suffering serious harm.

When I ask participants in my workshops to create name tags that identify all their various roles, at least 25 percent of all married women forget to include "wife." "Lover" only makes the list 15 percent of the time, and when it does, it's usually near the bottom.

But our relationships won't wait. We have numerous demands pulling and pushing on us, but that doesn't make it right or smart to shove our partners aside. The fact that we are so

quick to put our relationships on hold is just one more mani-
festation of our ambivalence. We don't want to commit, so we
come up with good reasons not to.

The inner battle between ambivalence and commitment
changes over time. Sometimes the shift to commitment is facilitated by a life-changing event—a death in the family, an experience when one's mate heroically rises to the occasion. Times
like these can cause paradigm shifts, when we suddenly and
spontaneously view things differently. A part of the wall falls
away and we find ourselves closer together, standing on the
same side. It's too bad we can't orchestrate such events, as they
are powerfully persuasive.

Fortunately, we *can* achieve the same end through a more
deliberate, rational process. The mind's ability to take in new
information—to register "Aha! I get it"—makes it possible for
an Inner Shift to occur simply because we have learned to think
about things in a new way.

Taking Responsibility

Making a commitment requires changing both our attitudes
(Inner Shifts) and our actions (Outer Moves). First we must take
responsibility for our part in putting up the wall, and then we
must actively alter our behavior. By *take responsibility,* I don't
mean *blame ourselves.* Blame, whether inner or outward directed, produces shame and keeps people stuck. Taking responsibility provides momentum for moving forward.

We may or may not be aware of the barriers we put up due
to our ambivalence. *Anger, sarcasm, and sexual unresponsive-
ness* are tangible ways we express a lack of commitment. Here
are other ways ambivalence is commonly played out:

Not making time for your mate.
Not listening or paying attention when he talks to you.
Discounting his opinions.

Refusing to spend time alone with him.

Leaving him out of important decision making.

Going to other people for most of your emotional needs.

Hanging on to anger even after amends are made.

If you're unclear about how you're sitting on the fence and what it's doing to your relationship, find out. Get some feedback. If this feels safe to you, ask your partner to share his perceptions of the subtle (and not so subtle) messages you send him. Or get input from a trusted friend who values your marriage and can be relatively objective. Another way to assess your behavior is to keep a journal—a week or two is enough— in which you record *every time* you sulk, blast him, complain about him to friends, or silently lower your expectations. Your goal isn't to feel bad about yourself, but to observe honestly your part in pushing him away.

Facing Your Own Issues

Taking responsibility also means taking a hard look at what's wrong or dysfunctional in our lives that has nothing to do with him—in other words, assessing ways we blame him for our unhappiness instead of dealing straight on with our own issues.

Many women—some experts estimate as many as 40 percent of the population—suffer from depression. Other women struggle with anxiety, fear, or generalized discontent stemming from a variety of problems. Financial stress, fatigue, work-related tensions, and other normal life pressures create discontent that naturally seeps into the marital relationship.

It's important to separate what's ours from what's his. This involves taking action, whether it's seeking professional assessment for depression, joining a women's group, or facing difficult decisions that may lead to greater peace and fulfillment.

When we avoid taking responsibility it costs us in two

ways—we mistakenly focus on him and we ignore our own problems—which won't get better and may, in fact, worsen without serious attention.

BREAKING THE CYCLE OF BEING SHORTCHANGED

Another way to take responsibility is to go backward in time to see exactly how we have built the wall. Chapter Two described a six-stage cycle that leads to becoming shortchanged. Let's look at that pattern again, this time from the perspective of healing.

At each stage we have closed certain doors in our relationship—doors that represent trust, compatibility, pleasure, and commitment. Now it's time to reverse the process. Imagine going back through each stage, carefully opening any doors that you are capable of at this point. Some you may be able to open fully; others you may only be able to peek through or open a crack. Still others may need to remain closed for the time being, and that's just fine. What's important for now is to approach each stage, this time replacing ambivalence with commitment.

STAGE ONE: ADDING UP THE HURTS

Old attitude and behavior. We track every disappointment. We experience a slow shift from loving him to blaming him.

New attitude and behavior. We commit to resolve disappointments when they happen, without mudslinging or martyrdom. We experience a slow shift from blaming him to expressing and letting go of our hurts when they happen.

STAGE TWO: BUILDING A CASE

Old attitude and behavior. We start to feel justified in our
   disappointment, anger, and hurt. We recount his failings
   to other people, keep a mental list, or throw his crimes
   back in his face.

New attitude and behavior. We see how we are trapping
   ourselves in disappointment, anger, and hurt. We stop
   saying bad things about him to other people, and
   recommit our energies to improving our relationship.

STAGE THREE: LOWERED EXPECTATIONS

Old attitude and behavior. As our list of grievances grows,
   we compensate by matching our expectations to the level
   of our experiences. We begin to disinvest in our
   relationships and seek to satisfy our needs elsewhere.

New attitude and behavior. As our commitment grows, we
   see tangible improvement in the way we feel toward our
   partner. We begin to approach the relationship with
   realistic optimism and hope.

STAGE FOUR: SMOLDERING ANGER

Old attitude and behavior. We overreact when he does
   something wrong and are blind to the good things that
   happen between us. We create a self-fulfilling prophecy
   of predictable disappointment.

New attitude and behavior. We express our anger
   constructively, with the goal of forgiveness and healing.
   This frees us to appreciate what is good in the
   relationship.

STAGE FIVE: ON THE FENCE

Old attitude and behavior. With one foot in, one foot out of the relationship, our predominant response to our mate is ambivalence. We are cautious, self-protective, and emotionally detached.

New attitude and behavior. In order to find out what is possible between ourselves and our mates, we plant both feet firmly in our relationships. We risk being open, vulnerable, and emotionally present.

STAGE SIX: SHORTCHANGED

Old attitude and behavior. We actively push him away. We are frosty, nasty, or simply resigned to our fate of a long-term, lukewarm relationship.

New attitude and behavior. We dare to invite him back into our lives because we genuinely believe our relationship will ultimately be satisfying and fulfilling.

We can break the cycle if we're willing to go back and see how we put up the wall and do whatever is necessary to take it down. This is a gradual process; whatever steps you take are steps in the right direction. But first, in order to take any steps at all, we have to be confident that our relationships are worth the risk.

PERSONAL CHECKPOINT

• Go back through the cycle of becoming shortchanged to discover where you've been in the past and where you are today. Determine what stage you are in now and decide if you can move backward in the cycle.

How Much Is Enough?

"Of course I'm committed. I'm still *here!*" women say, but the commitment is qualified by chronic feelings of dissatisfaction. We stay, but are never really happy. It's easier, safer, or more secure to settle than to make a firm commitment to love him or leave him.

Every relationship involves compromise, which is qualitatively different from "settling." Women who settle say, "I guess I'll stay, even though this is far less than what I want." Women who compromise say, "I choose to be with you, knowing full well who I am, who you are, what I'm giving and getting, what's possible, and what may never be." When we settle we feel powerless. When we compromise we feel powerful. We take an active hand in our destiny.

But before we can choose to be fully in our relationships, including making the necessary compromises, we need to know how much is enough. We need to clarify the bottom line: our personal and relationship goals, what we can and can't live without, what's urgent and what can wait. The goal of assessing the bottom line is to answer this question: *Is there enough of the right stuff to make it worthwhile to commit fully to my relationship?*

The following two questionnaires will help you figure out where you stand. Your answers will give you vital information on what's important to you, so that you can assess whether or not your relationship is meeting your bottom line. Section A explores your personal values and goals. Section B focuses on what matters most in your relationship.

SECTION A: WHAT DO YOU WANT OUT OF LIFE?

1. The three most important things in life are _____
_____.

2. I deeply care about _____
_____.

3. Being a good person means _____
_____.

4. Right now, I'm working on being _____
_____.

5. I feel satisfied with myself when I _____
_____.

6. My five-year personal goal is to _____
_____.

7. My fifteen-year personal goal is to _____
_____.

8. My ultimate personal goal is to _____
_____.

As you review your answers to each question, ask yourself: Does he understand who I really am and what matters to me? Does he support me in living up to my values and reaching my goals?

SECTION B: WHAT DO YOU WANT OUT OF YOUR RELATIONSHIP?

1. The key to a fulfilling relationship is _____
_____.

2. I am most peaceful with my partner when _____
_____.

3. The one thing I insist on from him is _____
_____.

4. I'm willing to compromise on _____
_____.

5. I'm not willing to compromise on _____
_____.

6. My five-year relationship goal is _____
_____.

7. My fifteen-year relationship goal is _____
_____.

8. My ultimate relationship goal is _____
_____.

As you answer each question in section B, ask yourself: Does my relationship satisfy—or come close to satisfying—my essential requirements?

Next, assess your bottom line and how well your mate satisfies it by answering these questions:

1. *Bottom line:* The minimum support I need from my mate in order to remain committed is _____

_____.

2. *Right now,* on a scale of 1 to 10, when it comes to supporting my personal and relationship goals, I'd say my mate falls above, below, or at my bottom line.

If your mate's support is above your bottom line, great! That means you are getting your fundamental needs met and can concentrate on fine-tuning your relationship. If he is at your bottom line, then you're doing fine. You may want more, but for now, there's enough support to warrant your continued commitment.

If your mate's level of support falls below your bottom line, you still have three choices:

1. You can leave.

2. You can resign yourself but stay in your relationship even though your bottom line isn't being met (settling).

3. You can choose to remain in your relationship, accepting the limitations, working on changing them, or both (compromise).

Whether you settle or compromise is largely a matter of attitude. You can remain interminably disappointed without doing anything about it. Or you can size up the situation, and make a powerful, positive choice. If you choose to compromise, then the ball is in your court. You make a commitment to live with what *is* and to stop whining about how you wish life could be. Like Sharon, whose story follows, you don't necessarily get everything you want, but you're satisfied by the compromise you've agreed to.

Sharon desperately wants to have another baby. Her daughter is turning four, and Sharon doesn't care to wait any longer.

Her husband, Al, is committed to building his career, which involves lots of travel. He is somewhat ambivalent about the costs—time, money, and stress—of a second child. However, he understands how important a baby is to Sharon, and so he is willing, somewhat grudgingly, to support her.

Al says, "If it were up to me, we wouldn't have another child. But I can see in Sharon's eyes how much she wants this, so I'm willing to go along. But she'll have to take care of it."

Sharon says, "I understand how Al feels. I'm willing to take on the brunt of the responsibility as long as I can have this baby."

Although she would prefer Al to be excited about the baby, she's willing to compromise, as long as he agrees to support them financially. Sharon's bottom line is a second child, even if she ends up being the sole care giver. "Sure, I'd rather that Al was one of these 'new father types' who diaper the baby and get up in the middle of night, but he's not. That doesn't have to keep either of us from having what we want."

Sharon could settle by foregoing her desire for a baby because she can't have it just the way she wants. Or she could settle by having the baby and then resenting Al's lack of parental involvement. Instead, she compromises by stating her bottom line and committing to accept what it takes to satisfy it.

It's important to remember that the bottom line is a starting point, not the last word on whether a relationship will make it. Knowing what our bottom line is gives us critical information on whether we can commit over the long haul.

Extending Our Time Line

Insisting that change happen *now* is a no-win proposition. When we give our partners the message that we're impatient, they feel more pressured and less capable of coming through. If we imply that our commitment only stands if they perform quickly—sort of a "limited-time offer"—they may quit before giving it a real chance.

"I'm not going to change overnight!" says thirty-five-year-old Eric, who has been in couples' counseling and group therapy for three years. Eric is obviously committed to working on his marriage, but he is equally adamant about wanting his wife, Ellie, to extend her time line and to acknowledge the distance he's come.

"When we got married I was totally in the dark about what it means to be a partner," admits Eric. "I came from a crazy family. From the time I was five, I lived with my grandmother. She loved me, but money was always a struggle, and she didn't have much left to give. Even when I was little I had to be 'the man' in the family. My grandfather drank and my grandmother was often upset. I can't count the times, once I got older, that I ended up having to comfort my grandmother or put my grandfather to bed.

"I was attracted to Ellie because she was so good at taking care of herself and everything else. When we got married, I had just gotten my first real job as an associate with a big law firm, and I thought that was enough. Meanwhile, Ellie did all the cooking, cleaning, bills, and social arrangements. She took care of me. She helped me edit my briefs and strategize on how to make partner at the firm.

"I had no idea how frustrated she was until Kevin was born," Eric says. "When the baby came, Ellie backed off from taking care of me. She says she got tired of having two children instead of a husband who helped with the baby, but at the time I didn't have a clue as to what was wrong.

"That's when we first became estranged, especially sexually. We hardly ever made love, and we finally landed in therapy where we're trying to work things out," he says. "Now I'm learning how to be a better husband and a better father on a consistent basis. I'm hoping that by the time I'm forty I'll be there, but it's going to take time. Meanwhile, I want to get away from this blame-and-shame crap. If I screw up, I don't want to feel like I've screwed up *everything,* like I've gone back to ground zero."

Eric needs more time to grow and to prove himself to Ellie. She needs to figure out how much longer she's willing to hang in there and what kind of progress will make her trust that her investment is paying off. A longer time line would help them both: it would give him more of a chance to mature and it would give her the opportunity to develop a new image of him and greater partnership between them. Eric needs more encouragement from Ellie in order to continue trying; Ellie needs evidence of Eric's growth in order to trust.

STRATEGY FOR EXTENDING YOUR TIME LINE

Tell yourself   "I am willing to invest _____ amount of time in order to see what is possible. During this time I will remain involved and optimistic."

Don't tell him   "Either you change by January 1st or I'm out of here."

Do tell him   "I need _____ amount of time to see that our relationship is changing."

The risk   He will interpret your desire as pressure or control and refuse to participate.

The reward   Less pressure and more hope of making positive changes.

PERSONAL CHECKPOINT

• Name the biggest change you'd like to see happen in your relationship. This may be a change you need to make, he needs to make, or you both need to make. What is your time line? Are you willing to extend it? If so, for how long? What concrete changes do you need to see in order to remain committed?

Making the Shift

When you're willing to move ahead, these four steps can facilitate your shift from ambivalence to commitment. And remember, you're doing this for yourself—because it feels better to commit than to sit on the fence.

1. *Entertain the Possibility (Inner Shift).* Let yourself imagine what it might be like to feel more committed to your mate. Envision warmth instead of resentment and anger. Picture a romantic scene or revitalization of your sexual relationship. You don't need to *do* anything. Simply allow yourself to fantasize.

2. *Imagine the Rewards (Inner Shift).* Write down all potential rewards. Include both concrete improvements (his washing the dishes, rubbing your neck, or taking care of the children without being asked) along with your deepest yearning for closeness and connection.

3. *Experiment (Outer Move).* Come up with five ways in which you can actually express feelings of increased commitment—and try them out. Here are some ideas:

    • Really listen when he talks to you.
    • Compliment him.
    • Find out something he wants and grant his wish.
    • Surprise him with a special outing.
    • Share something vulnerable that you've been withholding.

- Initiate lovemaking . . . and focus on his pleasure.
- Let the dishes sit.
- Tell him why you love him. Be explicit.

4. *Give It Time (Inner Shift and Outer Move).* Your efforts at acting more committed will yield results, but it might take more time than you think. Try to have reasonable expectations and be careful not to base your level of commitment on his response. Just because you've decided to try doesn't mean he'll suddenly be receptive. As Al-Anon members say: "You're responsible for the effort, not the outcome."

You know you're in the process of making the shift from ambivalence to commitment when *you experience a growing feeling of optimism about your relationship.*

NINE

FROM SELF-
VICTIMIZATION TO
EMPOWERMENT

I wasted so much time and energy blaming him for everything that went wrong in my life," says Caroline. "I was convinced that if he'd change, the sun would shine in a different way!"

Every time we blame *him* for our unhappiness, hold on to hurt, or resign ourselves to disappointment, we actively choose to stay stuck.

Calling self-victimization a choice may seem harsh or wrong, like "blaming the victim." How we feel *is* partially a result of how we have been treated. But here is a crucial distinction: Anger and self-protection are totally appropriate responses to violence and all forms of abuse, none of which should be tolerated in a relationship. If he crosses those lines, he is blameworthy. In such cases, staying focused on hurt or anger galvanizes us to get out of the victim role, a place no one belongs.

But assuming there is no threat of violence or abuse, we do victimize ourselves when we continue to focus on past hurts or fail to act on our own behalf. We become empowered by resolving hurt feelings, asking for what we want, and moving on.

PRODUCTIVE ANGER OR SPINNING YOUR WHEELS?

"It got to the point where my rage was more real than anything else in my relationship," admits Candice, who says she was mad at her husband, Eliot, for the first four years of their marriage. "He was always working. When I was pregnant, he missed over half of our childbirth classes, even though I told him how important it was for him to be there. When I went into labor, it took two hours to track him down. My mom had to take me to the hospital and he dashed in right at the last minute.

"After Emma was born, I totally shut Eliot out. When he talked to me I threw back one-word answers. If he tried to touch me, I'd give him this withering look. I refused to lose the extra twenty pounds I was carrying, because I figured if I kept the weight on, he'd stay away."

At first Candice's behavior toward Eliot was productive—her way of making sure her husband knew how angry she was. And it put her in the position of power. "My anger felt good," Candice admits. "He was knocking on *my* door for a change!"

After months of scorning Eliot, however, she tired of being the "rage monster." But by this time, anger was the main emotion in her repertoire, her most powerful defense weapon, and she clung to it long after it was needed.

"I knew Candy was pissed at me and I knew why," says Eliot. "I asked her to forgive me, but no matter what I said she was still upset. Those first few years I guess I *was* kind of a workaholic, especially during her pregnancy. I was oblivious to what she needed. But once I saw what was going on, I promised to make it up to her."

But Candy wasn't so quick to forgive. "I knew that if I stopped being angry I would open myself to being vulnerable and I wasn't ready for that," she says. "I was scared that if I let up, he would stop taking me seriously."

Initially, Candy succeeded in getting Eliot's attention, and he responded by trying to rectify the damage. But as time passed and Candy refused to forgive him, Eliot backed off. Candy simply wasn't ready to let go of what, for her, was a very painful experience; as the wronged party, she felt that healing needed to happen on her timetable. Meanwhile she and Eliot co-existed in a chilly standoff.

Candice's story points out why we're sometimes reluctant to make the shift from self-victimization to empowerment, especially when anger is involved. Painting ourselves as a victim and holding tight to our anger can be intoxicating. Anger is a big feeling; it makes us feel powerful and in control.

STRATEGY FOR LETTING GO OF ANGER

Tell yourself   "Underneath my anger is pain. I can choose to hold on to my anger in order to protect myself, or I can heal my pain."

Don't tell him   "I'll stop being angry when I'm good and ready."

Do tell him   "I am angry because of _____. In order to forgive and heal, I need more time or _____."

The risk   He may experience shame in the face of your anger and react by getting angry at you.

The reward   Relief and greater receptiveness toward your mate.

PERSONAL CHECKPOINT

•   What are you still angry about in your relationship? What
    are you getting out of holding on to your anger? What
    would it take for you to relinquish it?

I'M ANGRY SO HE MUST BE DOING SOMETHING WRONG

Sometimes we're angry and we don't know why.

"I can walk in the door at dinner time and tell just by
looking at Donna's back whether she's in a good mood or
whether she's mad and it's going to be a long night," says Jay.
"I used to take her on, but I've learned that her mood often
doesn't have anything to do with me. Either she's had it with
the kids or she's frustrated about something that happened at
work. I try to ignore her. Or, if she's really being awful, I'll tell
her to take a break and let me take over."

Jay is unusually accepting of Donna's volatile moods. Ben,
on the other hand, admits he's near the end of his rope in his
marriage to Esther. "I hate her outbursts, and I don't know what
to do about them anymore," he says quietly. "She's become
such an angry person, like a porcupine who attacks when you
come close. I've told her she needs to figure out why she's so
furious and do something about it or I'm going to leave."

Whether or not he is the direct cause of Esther's anger, Ben
is right in his assessment that it's up to her to resolve it. From his
perspective, her rage is ruining their relationship.

What does Esther say? "I'm out of control," she admits. She
goes on to say that she has even hit Ben, once striking him so
hard that his glasses flew across the room.

How can you tell when your anger is serving you, and when
it's getting in your way? This chart can help.

UNPRODUCTIVE ANGER	PRODUCTIVE ANGER
Is dumped.	Is expressed honestly.
Goes on and on.	Is finite.
Adds fuel to the fire.	Aims at resolution.
Is controlling.	Is empowering.
Feels draining.	Feels satisfying.

There are three common mistakes we make when expressing anger: *We justify, we dump, and we exaggerate.*

We think we need to rationalize our anger, but we don't. It's enough simply to say, "I'm angry . . ." without listing our reasons going all the way back to 1962. We justify because we don't really feel it's all right to be angry without developing an airtight case. But we actually do more damage by going on and on. It's much more powerful to make a simple, quiet statement and then leave it to him to respond.

When we dump, we throw in *all* the other things we're mad about instead of staying on the subject. This only confuses the issue and makes it more difficult for him to hear what we're saying. It gives him an excuse to dismiss us—"She's on the warpath again." And it pushes him farther away.

Our third common mistake—exaggerating in order to show him we mean it—means that we act angrier than we really are, embellishing our story or turning up the volume. This may get his short-term attention, but in the end, it will make him run for cover. Saying, "Listen, you jerk, I've been picking up the socks for the last twenty years, and I quit!" may get him to pick up his socks, but he'll probably throw them at you or sullenly stuff them in the hamper. No one likes being on the receiving end of angry outbursts; all they do is create defensiveness and more anger. Instead, you might say, "It makes me angry to see your socks lying there on the floor. Would you please pick them up?" He may still ignore your request, but he has less reason to.

Here are some tried-and-true strategies for expressing anger productively:

1. *Figure out what you're really angry about.* Don't say anything until you're sure what's bothering you.

2. *Speak, don't scream.* Acting reasonable and civilized strengthens your position.

3. *Scream, don't speak.* In relationships that thrive on dramatic scenes, acting reasonably can be infuriating to the other person. Instead, go ahead and give it your all, but be sure not to be violent or abusive.

4. *Stay on the subject.* Focus on a specific situation without throwing in other complaints.

5. *Don't say "never" or "always."* Resist making sweeping statements and blowing things out of proportion.

6. *Use an example.* Concrete illustrations (only one, please!) are helpful because they are easy to relate to.

7. *Separate the doer from the deed.* Make sure he knows that even though you're angry at his actions, you still love him.

8. *Get off the soapbox.* Most fights never get finished. Say what you have to say, listen to his response, see if there's a way to forgive, and then be done with it.

9. *Offer options.* Give him some suggestions of what he can do to repair the damage. This is *not* taking care of him; it's doing whatever possible to reconcile.

10. *Get help.* If your anger is eating you up and no matter what he does, you can't let go of it, seek outside help for yourself and your relationship.

REAL POWER

There's something better, sweeter, more powerful than anger, and that's *action*. Getting in touch with how we feel and what we want, and then going for it, is far more empowering than staying in a stew about him.

There are two parts to taking action: *stating how we feel* and *asking for what we want*.

Stating our feelings and having them acknowledged is key to empowerment. Safely saying, "This is who I am and this is what is going on with me," makes us feel respected as human beings. I am convinced most relationships will be profoundly improved if both partners feel free to express themselves without fear of judgment or blame.

This is difficult because intimate partners easily get enmeshed: We take on each other's problems and feel responsible for each other's feelings. She says, "I feel lonely." He hears, "You're not giving me what I need," which translates into, "If I'm not giving her what she needs then I must not be good enough." At this point, he either defends himself or deflects the problem back to her. All she wants is for him to listen; instead she gets a million reasons why she *shouldn't* be feeling what she's feeling.

In order to circumvent this mess, both partners need to *be quiet and listen*. Taking turns talking is a good idea. Knowing we can count on ten uninterrupted minutes to say our piece makes it easier to get to the point. And knowing that we'll get our turn if we're patient helps us be a better audience.

One effective technique is to express "positive intentions."[1] If you need to express anger or disappointment about something in your relationship, try to follow up with a statement that conveys your genuine desire to get along better. For example, if you say, "I'm feeling upset that you've gone to meetings three nights this week," then add your positive intention: "It's important to tell you this because I miss you and want us to spend more time together."

When you say how you feel and what you want, make sure your mate knows your positive intention. Let him know that you just want him to listen, not to fix problems or defend himself.

THAWING OUT

Sexuality is one area in which women commonly feel victimized, or at least, mistrustful. Asserting ourselves sexually— knowing what we want and asking respectfully—is such hard work that we may easily give up, pushing him away instead of pushing through our resistance.

Anger, fear, and stress are all reasons why we freeze him out. We're cold. We don't initiate sex. We may not even be willing to let him touch us, co-existing as roommates rather than lovers.

We lose so much when we're unwilling or unable to enjoy physical intimacy with our partners! We deprive ourselves of physical warmth and passion that could be immeasurably healing.

"I want to have a better sexual relationship, but I just don't feel safe," explains Betsy, who says that her seven-year marriage to Roger is nearly perfect except for the fact that they rarely make love. "We start out okay," she says. "We give each other backrubs, we make out a little, but as soon as he makes an overtly sexual move, I freeze. I go from wanting him to wanting nothing to do with him."

"Sometimes Betsy just flat out doesn't want to be touched— but she doesn't say anything," Roger says, in turn. "I get the motor cranked up, but then she starts acting weird and I can tell she doesn't want to be doing this, so I stop. But it bothers me. I feel like saying, 'Screw you. Why didn't you just say what you wanted in the first place?'

"I know she's had bad experiences, but sometimes I feel like I'm in bed with a whole lineup of other men. I've never taken advantage of her. I'm doing my damndest to love her and I'm getting lumped in with some other guy who 'done her wrong.'"

"It's not Roger's fault," Betsy adds, "but I get freaked out when there he is, all hot and bothered, and all I want is to be held. He starts coming on to me and I panic. I feel violated. Then we get into an awful fight; he says I'm frigid or calls me a 'tease,' I clam up and we retreat to our own sides of the bed. Most of the time I just turn over and pretend I'm sleeping to avoid a scene."

Betsy's strategy is extremely successful at heading off her husband's passes. The trouble is, it's equally successful at keeping her from getting the warmth and satisfaction she needs. Her conviction that she won't get what she wants prevents her from getting anything at all. Her intense feelings of pressure preclude imagining what it would be like to be aroused or fulfilled.

For Betsy to make the shift from self-victimization to empowerment, she needs to trust that Roger can provide her with sexual pleasure in a way that doesn't frighten her. She needs to tune in to her inner resistance, becoming aware of exactly how and why she turns off.

To this end, I led Betsy through a guided imagery of a typical night in bed with her husband. In her imagery, Betsy and Roger talked for a while, and then curled up together. They began kissing. But when she imagined Roger sliding his leg between hers, she visibly tensed.

"What's going on?" I asked.

"I'm scared," she said.

"What are you scared of?"

"I know he wants sex and I'm afraid to say no," she replied.

"How do you know what he wants?" I countered, suggesting she check out her assumption.

She was right. She asked Roger what he wanted, and he told her he wanted to make love. "What do *you* want?" I asked.

"I want him to stop moving so fast and just hold me."

"Tell him that," I suggested, and in her imagery, she did.

Her shoulders relaxed, and tears began to form in the corners of her eyes. "What's happening?" I asked softly.

"Roger is holding me. I feel safe."

"What do you want now?" I asked.

"To make love with my husband," she whispered.

If I had asked Betsy before the guided imagery why her sexual relationship continually jammed, she would have said it was all "Roger's fault." She would have defended her strategy of withholding, explaining it was the only way to protect herself. In truth, Betsy didn't really want Roger to go away or stop touching her; she simply wanted to express her sexuality on her own terms. Once she felt safe to do so, the thought of making love turned from pressure to pleasure.

LETTING HIM IN

Lovemaking can go a long way toward healing our relationships. Acknowledging the willingness to be more sexual is a statement that we're serious about taking down the wall.

Once again, the best reason to reinvest is for our own sakes. We need physical nurturing and pleasure in order to flower fully as human beings. We owe it to ourselves and our partners to try—even if it means sometimes pushing ourselves to participate when we're distracted or afraid. We may need to consciously choose to be sexual in order to get past initial resistance to a place where we feel good.

If we're too stressed out to make time or shift gears, "one thing that helps women relax is to tune in to their bodies instead of their heads," sex therapist Dr. Constance Avery-Clark suggests. She advises women to pay attention to their sensual feelings in the here and now. "If you're lying there and he's caressing your shoulder, pay attention to how that feels instead of thinking about the bills and the laundry and the report that's due on Monday. Let yourself be immersed in the experience."

Easier said than done? "If I'm not into it, I'm not into it," says Sally, expressing the thoughts of many women. She asks: "How am I supposed to psyche myself into wanting it when it's the last thing I'm interested in?"

What can Sally do to change how she's feeling about making love? Both Inner Shifts and Outer Moves can help her to overcome her lack of desire.

Considering these three points can help you make an Inner Shift from resistance to receptivity:

1. What is my resistance made of? Am I tired? Angry? Distracted? Is there anything going on between us that needs to be dealt with before I can be sexually open?

2. Can I imagine getting anything good out of making love? Can I remember what it's like to feel aroused? Can I recall feeling peaceful and content afterward?

3. When have I felt this way before? Was there anything I did or he did that helped my resistance melt away?

If your answers on the first point bring up static that's getting in the way of the trust it takes to make love, then you have two choices: Deal with it and get it out of the way or table it for later discussion. (If you choose the latter, then you really have to be able to put it away for the moment so you can focus on making love.)

If fatigue, distraction, or other normal stresses are making it difficult to shift gears into a sexual mind-set, then go on to points two and three. Your answers on point two reveal whether you can remember how good sex can feel. In order to overcome resistance successfully you need to see some potential rewards. You have to be able to imagine something positive coming out of lovemaking, otherwise it seems futile to summon the effort.

Your answers on point three are the bridge to making Outer Moves. If you really think back, you may recall how you've broken through resistance in the past. If something has worked for you, try it again. For example, you may remember, "Oh yes, the last time I felt turned off like this it was because my husband was coming at me so fast I felt as if we were in a marathon. So I asked him to stop for a minute and just be with me. We put music on and I concentrated on breathing and relaxing my body until I was ready." Or "When I start to freeze, I fast-forward to remember the sensation of the last instant before orgasm. If I can imagine it, I am usually willing to hang in long enough to get aroused."

Here's a practical list to draw on when you want to have sex (either because you'd enjoy it, because you know your relationship needs it, or both), but your mind and/or body are less than agreeable:

Meditate

Close your eyes and imagine tensing and then relaxing every part of your body. Pay attention to how you feel.

Masturbate

Take a warm bubble bath or lie in bed alone and get yourself in the mood. Props are permitted. A vibrator or erotic book may be just the right touch.

Fantasize

Star in a steamy fantasy. Never mind if he's a bit player or altogether absent. Reach for the stars. Ultimately, both of you benefit.

Initiate

If *you* make the moves, you have greater control over the tone, speed, and style of lovemaking. Initiating also gets your mind off of yourself and more focused in the here and now.

Set the scene   Candles, music, mirrors, or other "mood en-
hancers" can help you make the transition
from the day's demands to a romantic rendezvous.

Make the time   Don't wait for the perfect moment. Seize the
opportunity when it presents itself, when
you're still fresh and in the mood, even if it
means turning off the TV or trying new and
different times to be together.

Fast-forward   Concentrate on remembering exactly how it
feels when it feels good. To do this, consciously turn down the voice inside that
says: "But I'm tired," "But the living room
needs vacuuming," "But I have to be up in
six hours." Instead, think: "This is going to
feel terrific."

Just do it   If you can go along for the ride—you may
end up enjoying yourself despite your reservations.

Because many women find it virtually impossible to make
love when serious unresolved feelings are hanging in the air,
this may not be a realistic option for everyone. If sex is one of
these serious problems, you just may not be able to make love
and still feel safe. However, physical intimacy—if you're willing
to make the leap of faith and let him in a little—often paves the
way for forgiveness and reconciliation.

Most women report that lovemaking actually makes them
feel more loving toward their mates. "When we haven't done it
for a long time, I forget how it feels!" says Leslie. "At first I can't
remember why I'd want to go to all the trouble. But then we do it,
and afterward I almost always say, 'That was great! Why don't we
do that more often?' Being sexual with Seth makes our whole

relationship more peaceful. We like each other more. We get along better. We're more willing to go through the hard times."

Asking for what we want—in bed or out—is the next step in empowerment. Traditionally, women have a hard time naming and asking for what we want. We have been conditioned to put our needs aside, to dismiss them or consider them irrelevant.

"I never thought in terms of what I wanted until I was nearly thirty years old," says Arlinda, whose fresh-faced appearance belies a gritty realism and keen sense of irony. The youngest in her family, with three older brothers, she learned early on to keep her opinions and desires to herself—behavior she carried into her marriage.

STRATEGY FOR LETTING IN SEXUAL INTIMACY

Tell yourself   "I need and deserve sexual warmth, pleasure, and intimacy."

Don't tell him   "I've got my mind on that meeting tomorrow."

Do tell him   "I want to be more sexual with you, but _____ is getting in the way. It would help if we could _____."

The risk   Depending on how often you withhold sexually, he may criticize or shame you when you're already feeling vulnerable.

The reward   A pleasurable sexual relationship that builds trust and intimacy between you.

"Once my therapist told me to stand on one foot in the corner. She said, 'Tell me when you need help.' I stood there for twenty-five minutes! Finally, she said, 'What are you going to do—wait until your leg breaks? And *then* who are you going to be mad at?' "

Slowly, Arlinda has learned to ask for what she wants. She still has to force herself to do it. "It's hard," she says. "First you have to know what you want, and then you have to have enough self-worth to do something about it. Asking is risky. I have to be vulnerable and risk not getting what I want even though I *have* asked."

THE ART OF ASKING

The ABCs of effectively requesting what we want are *asking respectfully, being specific,* and *cultivating detachment.*

In his best-selling book *All I Really Need to Know I Learned In Kindergarten,* Robert Fulghum offers "rules" for getting along in life. Impressed by his advice, I asked my own kindergartner, Evan, for words of wisdom before I embarked on a recent business trip. "Remember to say please and thank you," he told me. I'm sure Fulghum would gladly add these to his list.

Saying please and thank you works because human beings like to be treated graciously. It works with your mate because it disarms him, just when he is prepared for an onslaught, not a polite request he can honor or refuse.

Be sure, however, that you're very specific. Spell out exactly what you want, in tangible terms. Generalities are overwhelming. Saying "I want you to start loving me," even if we tack on please and thank you, doesn't give our partners a clue as to where to begin. Saying, "Please rub my neck" or "I'd like you to look at me when we're talking" is something he can handle.

A participant in one of my workshops complained that her husband never helped. "Have you asked him?" I wanted to know.

"Sure," she replied. "I've told him a million times that he never helps."

"Tell me five ways he could help you," I instructed her, which she listed in a flash. "Now pick one and put it in the form of a request."

She snarled and said, "It would be nice if you'd fold the laundry once every couple of years."

"That's a reprimand, not a request," I reminded her and asked her to try again.

This time she said, "I'd appreciate if you'd vacuum the house once a week." The woman went home and tried it out. Her husband, surprised at being asked politely to do something he could easily do, agreed to vacuum. A few days later, *he* asked what he could do to help her.

Of course, things don't always turn out this way. Vicky, who's been married to Carlos for three years, has repeatedly made two requests: fresh flowers every once in a while and a monthly date when they get a baby-sitter and go to a movie.

"That sounds doable," I suggested to Carlos.

He agreed, but then went on to explain why he won't satisfy Vicky's seemingly simple request. "Vicky wants romance—walks on the beach, candlelit dinners—and I'm just not that kind of a guy," he explained. "I don't want to spend the money and I don't see any reason to do something so out of character just to please her."

Carlos *says* he loves Vicky and is committed to her. He knows what she wants and, still, he refuses to come through. What's going on?

The two are locked in a power struggle between what she wants and what he's willing to give. Even though Carlos agrees that their marriage could use a little romance, he's not willing to do it exclusively her way. He won't bend on this—not as long as he feels pressured to be someone other than who he is. HE needs room to make an active choice—to give because he *wants* to, not because he feels backed into a corner.

Vicky can help by asking for what she wants in a new way: She can ask him simply to do it *for her, just because it would make her happy.* This allows Carlos room to *choose* to satisfy his wife without changing his style or compromising his identity.

STRATEGY FOR ASKING RESPECTFULLY

Tell yourself   "I have the right to ask for anything I want. I may or may not get it."

Don't tell him   "If you loved me, you'd ＿＿＿＿＿."

Do tell him   "I'd really like it if you'd ＿＿＿＿＿. It's very important to me and would make me feel good."

The risk   He may flat out refuse or give lip ser-vice but still not change.

The reward   Getting what you want.

PERSONAL CHECKPOINT

- Is there something you've asked for repeatedly in your relationship but not gotten? How are you phrasing your request? Are you presenting it as an ultimatum or couching it in terms of disappointment? Or are you asking for what you want in terms of why it's important to you?

CULTIVATING DETACHMENT

Even if we ask respectfully we may not get what we want, which is why it's essential to cultivate detachment—to be realistic about what he can and can't, will and won't give and not to overreact each time he fails to comply.

Detachment doesn't mean that what we're asking for doesn't matter; it matters a great deal or we wouldn't be asking. It simply means we have perspective. We accept that what we want doesn't have to happen on our time schedule. We know that neither our survival nor our serenity depend on it, and we're willing to wait.

This scale is a useful tool for figuring out what's critical and what's not, what's urgent and what can wait. On the left hand are six categories, increasing in importance. Each category combines urgency of change (desirable, important, or critical) with a time frame (soon or right now).

Choose three things you want to see changed in your relationship and look at where they fall on the scale:

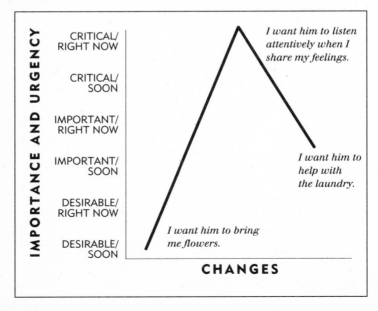

Because it's easy to feel that everything is critical and needs to change "yesterday," applying the changes you want in your relationship to this scale helps to prioritize them. Whatever falls in the highest part of the graph deserves immediate attention. Changes that fall in the middle range are important and need to be actively worked on, but not in an atmosphere of urgency. The lower points are generally longer-term changes that you should be aware of, but won't make or break your relationship. These changes are worth working on, but within a more leisurely time frame.

HITTING A WALL

The one question women ask all the time is: "What if I ask and ask and he still won't change?"

What if you do everything you can—ask respectfully, be specific, cultivate detachment—and you still don't get anywhere?

Before you throw in the towel, here are four serious questions to ask yourself:

1. *Is there anything else I can do?* Have I done everything possible to approach him in a way that ensures getting what I want? Use your creativity. If there's anything—*anything*— you can do to communicate more effectively or make it more possible for him to come through, try it! Working to find a successful way to approach your mate isn't the same as pandering to him. Your goal is to do your best for your own sake.

2. *Is my timetable flexible?* Is it urgent, or can it wait? Can I make a contract with my partner that would respect both of our timetables and make change more possible?

3. *Where else can I get what I want?* Is it possible to get *some* but not all of what I want from him? Is there any part that

can be satisfied elsewhere without jeopardizing our relationship? There are many things you can and should get outside your relationship. Stimulation, companionship, and enjoyment can come from many different quarters, including careers, children, and friendships. Women who want their husbands to be more emotionally forthcoming often find they can get some of that from close friendships with other people, most often other women. However, if *most* or *all* of your intimacy is generated outside the marriage, then it's natural to ask what you are getting that makes it worth staying.

4. *How important is this?* Is this a relationship *breaker* or a relationship *enhancer*? Is what I want critical to my happiness, or is it something that would be nice, but that I can live without? Think about your bottom line and remember: Successful relationships necessitate compromise. However, if you're compromising your integrity, values, or most sacred vision of intimacy, you're actually settling, in which case you need to reevaluate whether it's worth it to you to stay together.

WHEN NOTHING CHANGES

Let's say you *truly* have made the commitment. You've tried everything—including going to counseling. You believe, deep in your heart, that you've given your relationship your very best shot. Yet nothing has changed but *you*. He isn't any different. The same problems still exist, trust is nonexistent, and hope is waning.

Ending a relationship is a heart-wrenching decision. Regardless of the circumstances, leaving someone we once loved, and perhaps still love, is terribly painful. While I would never advise anyone to separate or divorce without knowing everything about her particular situation, these are the facts: If you've made a commitment, if you've shifted from self-victimization to power, then you're probably feeling strong. That strength can guide you to make the decision that's right for you. Maybe it's choosing to stick with your relationship for now, even if it's unsatisfying and unfulfilling. Maybe it's leaving your relationship behind and getting on with your life and having the possibility of new relationships.

Most women who say good-bye do so only after prolonged attempts to save the relationship. "I hung in until the bitter end," says Debra, "until I was absolutely positive that staying with him would destroy me spiritually, if not physically.

"For the first six years or so, Ethan and I got along pretty well. We were both really independent, and we didn't expect much from each other. But then our daughter was born with a heart defect. I needed Ethan, not just for moment-to-moment help, although Holly required huge sums of energy and constant maintenance, but mostly I needed him to talk to. To hold me.

"When our second child was born, all our intimacy went right down the tubes. I was wrapped up in the kids, and Ethan didn't seem to understand that I needed some nurturing too. He just went away. He had a catatonic routine—I'd be talking to him and he'd get this blank stare on his face. He controlled me through his silence. Once he didn't say anything for ten days. I'd leave and walk up and down the block crying. I'd try to tell him I was unhappy, that we needed to support each other, and he'd tell me I was nuts. That I needed too much.

"I felt like I was sitting on the fence and the fence was ripping me apart. The more aware I became of the pain, the harder it was to maintain the charade. It meant giving up the American Dream, which was hard to do, especially because I'd grown up Catholic. You're always married in the eyes of the Catholic Church. My friends would say, 'How can you leave Ethan? You have the perfect marriage!'

"But I couldn't keep it up. There was no hope anymore. No trust. But I felt trapped, until the night I had the dream.

"I dreamed that I was wandering in the desert. It was extremely hot . . . endless dunes . . . blazing sun. I had a canteen with one inch of water left. I'd been conserving this water for days and I felt like I was near the end, but I had to keep stumbling. I came to the top of a dune and looked out over the edge. I saw a red hand pump. I was sure it was a mirage. Waves of heat shimmered against the surface of the sand. The red pump turned blue, its shape distorted and zigzaggy.

"I went down to investigate and saw it was not a mirage. It was real. There were lime deposits around the base so I knew there had to be water. But I pumped and pumped and nothing came out. It just clanked. I looked at my one inch of water and stood there the longest time debating what to do. Should I put in my one inch of water to prime the pump? What if it wasn't enough? Or should I keep my inch of water and try to make it out? Slowly I took my canteen and walked off across the desert.

"When I awoke from the dream, I was elated," recalls Debra. "I knew I had nothing left to give the marriage. It was time to save my own life."

Debra's powerful dream made it possible for her to make the right decision. In the three years since their divorce, she has grown tremendously. "I've learned to listen to my heart, to trust myself. I'm not ready for another relationship, I'm afraid of being hurt again, but at least I know what I'm looking for. The kind of marriage I want is a partnership in serving God," says Debra. "Anything less isn't worth the effort."

HOW DO YOU KNOW IF IT'S TIME TO LEAVE HIM?

There's no way to be absolutely sure. The decision to divorce is enormous and involves so much loss and grieving that certainty comes only with time. I know, both from personal experience and from hearing women's stories, that breaking marriage vows breaks hearts, no matter how many reasons we repeat to ourselves to confirm the necessity of doing it. Witnessing our children's pain; counting the years of effort, investment, and shared hopes that will never be realized; and sifting through treasured memories and photographs of happier times make it impossible to come to such a monumental decision without some degree of doubt. That doubt, although agonizing, is proof positive of how much we've loved and how much we are giving up.

So what does it take to be reasonably resolved in the face of such loss? Here's what women say who have been through it. You know it's time to say good-bye:

- If you hate how you are when you're with him.
- If being with him is destroying your health, self-esteem, or capacity to be loving.
- If you can't stand to have him touch you anymore.
- If you've tried counseling and still can't resolve your most central issues.
- If you'd rather be alone than be with him.
- If you believe your children will be better off in the long run.
- If you know that it's no longer worth the effort.
- If you fantasize about his disappearing or dying.
- If you've asked him for what you *really* want and he hasn't come through.
- If you've done what *he's* asked for (within reason) and it hasn't helped.
- If you've confronted your fears of being alone and are still willing to do it.
- If you'd tell your best friend to leave in the same situation.
- If you've looked hard at what you're losing and know it's worth the trade-off.

- If you've prayed and made peace with yourself that he is not meant to be your spiritual partner for life.

- If your dreams have died.

MAKING OVERTURES

While Debra's story illustrates a time to end a marriage, Mimi's story is turning out very differently. After a torturous few years of vacillating between staying and leaving, she has made tentative steps toward building a better relationship.

"My anger in my marriage built up over years and years," begins Mimi, telling the saga of her fifteen-year marriage, separation, and near divorce. "Nick turned out to be so different from the man I thought I had married. It was like living with an alien, that's how far apart we were. I cared about politics and he was totally apathetic. I wanted to share so many things and he couldn't talk about feelings for more than five minutes without changing the subject.

"But there were some great things about our relationship. We were very attracted to each other and the sex was good. We both had successful careers, and we were great 'business partners.' We had lots of friends and we liked doing many of the same things. But half the time I felt empty, as if I were living with someone who would never understand me, never give me what I needed.

"I'd consider leaving, and then I'd look around at my friends who were single or divorced and I'd think, 'I'd have to be stupid to give up what I have.' I didn't want to give up everything just because Nick wasn't everything I wanted. I didn't want to give up and then live to regret it."

Instead of giving up, Mimi went into therapy, and there she began to question everything: her values, her upbringing, what she wanted in life. "As I got to know myself better, I started to say, 'Oh, I believe this' or 'I don't agree with that.' I became more confident about the kind of person I am."

Because everything in Mimi's life was subject to scrutiny, she anguished over whether or not to remain married. She and Nick separated for six months, during which time Mimi assessed her feelings. "For months I had a wrenching feeling in my stomach," she says. "I tried to allow myself to feel my anger instead of fighting it. I journaled and journaled and walked and walked, trying to sort everything out. I forced myself to fantasize divorcing Nick, down to the details, including how we would work out our debts.

"In therapy I screamed and pounded my fists at my rage at my parents for having really loused up my childhood. They *never* let me express any anger. Now I couldn't *stop* feeling angry."

Once Mimi separated her anger at her parents from her anger at Nick, she was clearer about where she stood in her marriage. "I laid it on the line," she says. "I told Nick that things had to change or that was it. I decided to give it six more months.

"Standing up for myself and saying what I wanted was incredibly freeing," says Mimi. "I asked him to pay more attention to my feelings. He said he'd try, but that I shouldn't expect miracles. He agreed to talk more, but we're still working on the emotional stuff. He gets scared and withdraws. But it's been four months and on the whole, things are considerably better."

By refocusing on herself, Mimi was able to transform her feelings toward Nick dramatically. "I no longer blame Nick for what happens to me," she explains. "Now when I'm angry or unhappy, I look inside and figure out what I can do to feel better. Sometimes that involves asking him to change. Other times it means I have to change to become happier with myself, which, of course, makes me happier with Nick."

Mimi's story is inspiring because it reveals what's possible if we're willing to stop being victims and start acting on our own

behalf. In order to understand the process, let's list the steps
Mimi took in coming to terms with her marriage:

1. She acknowledged her anger and admitted she was
   unhappy.
2. She took responsibility and sought professional help.
3. She searched deeply for her own identity and clarified her
   values.
4. She released her childhood rage.
5. She figured out her bottom line.
6. She decided on a deadline.
7. She asked for what she wanted.
8. She made compromises.

Mimi's turning point came when she began to define herself on her own terms, instead of blaming Nick and letting him
determine her happiness. In turn, she had to stop seeing him as
her oppressor, which meant accepting him as a fragile human
being. This ended up empowering them both.

Expressing how we feel and what we want can transform
our relationships because we give up control in exchange for
real power. We stop hanging on to our hurt and anger and start
enacting our own vision for a more fulfilling partnership.

You know you're in the process of making the shift from self-
victimization to empowerment if *you have stopped blaming him
and are ready to begin asking for what you want and need.*

FROM ADVERSARIES TO ALLIES

At our temple, it is customary for couples about to be married to be blessed during Friday night services. I recently watched one young couple stand hand-in-hand in front of the ark where the Torah is kept. They appeared to listen intently to the rabbi, searching for wisdom and guidance. He spoke of his hopes for them, about wanting them to love and support one another, saying, "May you grow together, become strong in one another, become united through common purpose and faith."

For me, the rabbi's words were a reminder of what marriage is meant to be—and how easily we fall off course, stop being on the same team. It's easy to fall into an adversarial position, blaming each other for what goes wrong in our lives. The clutch goes out in the car and it's *his* fault for procrastinating about getting a tune-up. It's midnight, there's no milk, and he's furious at *you* for forgetting to stop at the store. More serious problems—not enough money, a sick child, a fallout with close friends—precipitate finger-pointing brawls in which you're both convinced that it must be the other person's fault.

The shift from adversaries to allies means that instead of working against each other, we begin working together. Being allies means we can count on each other—absolutely—for support. It means that we stop consuming valuable energy proving who's to blame, and instead harness a mutual desire to work together on having a better relationship.

There are four essential elements to being a strong ally in an intimate relationship: *support, cooperation, mutual respect,* and *appreciation.*

SUPPORT, NOT ADVICE

We all want closeness with someone who takes our ups and downs personally, who revels in our success and bolsters us when we flounder. The catch is, we want our partners to provide unqualified support without throwing their own feelings and needs into the equation. This can be a difficult task, as Anne and Will have discovered.

"If I wanted your opinion, I'd ask for it!" Will snaps, disgustedly slamming his fist down on the kitchen table. He's just finished telling his wife, Anne, about his poor performance review. His employer has put him on probation and is withholding any raise until his work visibly improves.

Anne is scared that Will may lose his job and angry at him for blowing it. On the pretext of being interested in his feelings, she asks leading questions, but what she really wants is answers to assuage her own anxiety. Although she tries to appear composed, it sounds as if she's attacking him.

"Well, *have* you been falling down on the job?" she asks pointedly. She paces back and forth, stops and asks, "Couldn't you have talked him out of the probation?" Cradling her head in her hands, she sighs, "How are we ever going to make ends meet?"

Naturally Will resents Anne's line of questioning. He feels lousy and could use a little reassurance. He was looking for a cheerleader; instead, he gets the third degree.

When something happens that threatens us, our knee-jerk reaction is to pull out our support and protect ourselves. Instead of saying, "I know you must be scared about the money and so am I," as Anne might have done, we criticize, saying, "How could you have gotten us into this situation?" The only possible response is a defensive one, and so the battle lines are drawn.

Let's look at this situation from the other side. When we're down, all we really want is understanding. Right then we're not in the market for tips on how we might have handled things better. When we're vulnerable, advice translates into criticism no matter how well meaning it may be. We may be open to feedback later, but for now we want our partners to be sensitive to what *we* need, not to what would make *them* feel better.

PERSONAL CHECKPOINT

• When your mate turns to you for support, do your fear and anxiety get in the way? Is there anything you can do to become more responsive?

Here are three steps to help you put your own issues aside and be a more supportive ally:

1. *Pay attention (Inner Shift).* For the next twenty-four hours, notice any time your partner complains or shares a difficult issue he's dealing with.

2. *Just listen (Inner Shift and Outer Move).* It's the hardest thing in the world, but fight the temptation to criticize or offer advice unless it's specifically requested.

3. *Ask what you can do (Outer Move).* Find out how you can help—specific ways you can take some of the pressure off your partner or ease him through a difficult time.

COOPERATION

Most of us enter into our love relationship thinking of it as a partnership. But the spirit of cooperation fades as we begin to compete over who makes the decisions, whose career comes first, whose family we will spend the holidays with, and who gets to enjoy that most precious commodity of all—rest and relaxation.

Scarcity of time and energy creates a perception that life is a zero-sum game in which each partner's needs are seen as a direct threat to the other's being satisfied. Instead of championing each other, we become opponents. Our home becomes a war zone instead of a sanctuary.

Cooperation involves more than changing how we perceive our mates. It requires a transformation in our world view from one of scarcity to one of abundance. If we perceive the world as a frightening place in which we must scramble furiously to get what we need, we become stingy and Scrooge-like, in both giving and receiving love. We become overly concerned with protecting what we see as "finite" resources, when, in fact, we have an infinite capacity to love.

Allysa's Story

Adam felt invisible as he stood in a corner watching his wife, Allysa, hold court. It was "Spain Month" at their gourmet club for couples, and Allysa had spent hours in the kitchen preparing paella.

People just gravitate toward her, Adam thought, watching his wife surrounded by friends. He admired her outgoing personality, but had begun to resent all the attention she attracted. Things had gotten worse, it seemed, since she had won the nomination for state senator from their district.

There was an air of festivity as everyone sat down around the antique oak dining room table. Ron, their neighbor and this month's host, clinked his glass and called out, "How about a toast to our neighborhood celebrity?" "Here, here!" everyone clamored.

Adam sat back slightly from the table and got what Allysa had come to recognize as his "here-we-go-again" look. Then he excused himself and went outside for some air.

"All anyone talks about anymore is this damn campaign," Adam muttered to himself. "The phone rings every five minutes. You'd think she was running for president the way people carry on."

A tenured faculty member at a respected junior college, Adam has found a comfortable niche. His job isn't high-profile, at least not off campus, but he likes it. He doesn't envy Allysa her glamorous career, but lately he feels shoved into the background.

But he isn't out of the limelight for long. Three weeks into the campaign, her opponent unearths the fact that Allysa had an abortion sixteen years ago. She is publicly challenged to defend her decision. A story runs in the newspaper and Allysa starts getting vicious phone calls and letters, one calling her "a baby killer."

Although Adam can see that Allysa is under tremendous strain, he gives her little support. The abortion, which took place when Allysa unintentionally became pregnant a few months after their son was born, is still a sore spot between them. She insisted that having the baby would destroy her chance to graduate from law school and become an attorney. He acquiesced, but never really forgave her for depriving him of another child.

Allysa's campaign manager calls an emergency meeting to decide how she should respond. They draft a statement for the press. Allysa and her campaign manager feel it's imperative that Adam appear at her side during the press conference as a show of unity and support.

Adam is torn. Part of him wants Allysa to win, but he's still angry about the abortion. What he really wishes is that she would withdraw from the race and stop exposing their private affairs to the public eye.

Allysa needs Adam's support, emotionally and practically, but she's not going to softpedal in order to get it. The last thing she wants is to quit. And she isn't interested in rehashing the abortion right now, even though that might make Adam more willing to stand by her.

Adam *does* decide to show up at the press conference, but stands sullenly to the side. When a reporter asks how he feels about the abortion he replies: "Since when do my feelings count?" Mortified, Allysa confronts him immediately after the press conference. She breaks down crying and tells him how much she needs him right now. He realizes that he hasn't been feeling needed at all, and in fact, that's a big part of the problem. They slowly take the first step toward becoming allies and she swallows her pride and he finally comes through with love and support. For the first time, Adam sees Allysa's potential victory as his own, with tangible, shared rewards.

Life is hard enough without being adversarial with our mates. We need each other. Becoming allies means we recommit to work together toward a common end. It means we stop measuring our worth by comparison and enlist each other's support and cooperation, fortifying the bonds between us. Alfie Kohn, in his book *No Contest: The Case Against Competition,* says, "Cooperation sets things up so that by helping you I am helping myself at the same time. Our fates are linked. We sink or swim together."[1]

TOWARD A SPIRIT OF COOPERATION

How do you know whether you and your mate are competitive or cooperative? Check A or B on each of these questions:

Do you:
1. A. Celebrate his successes?
   B. Downplay his successes?
2. A. Resolve problems mutually?
   B. Walk away in the middle of fights?

3. A. Share important information?
   B. Withhold important information?
4. A. Build him up to other people?
   B. Criticize him to other people?
5. A. Trust his motives?
   B. Feel suspicious of him?
6. A. Inspire and encourage him?
   B. Discourage him from following his dreams?

STRATEGIES FOR COOPERATION

Tell yourself "My mate and I are on the same team."

Don't tell him "I can do it all myself. I've learned not to depend on you for anything."

Do tell him "I'd like us to cooperate with each other by _____."

The risk Giving more than you get.

The reward A winning team.

The more A's you have, the higher your Cooperation Quotient. If you mostly answer B, then try some of the following steps to enhance your cooperativeness:

1. *CELEBRATE his success.* Mark his triumphs by sending flowers, planning a special dinner, or scrawling a congratulatory note in soap on the bathroom mirror.

2. *PERSEVERE.* Get in there and fight for your relationship. Getting through hard times together is a real victory.

3. *GIVE him ALL the information.* Make a point of filling him in, either by posting notes in a central location, making regular dates to catch up, or sharing choice entries from your journal.

4. *PROMOTE him.* Be a good press agent, and be sure to show him his clippings. If you can't think of nice things to say about him, don't say anything.

5. *TRUST him.* Treat him as if you assume he has your best interests at heart.

6. *NURTURE his dreams.* Let him know that you want him to achieve his goals. Take him seriously.

Naturally, he needs to do all of the same things in order for the two of you to become allies. Although you can work toward having a more cooperative spirit yourself, ultimately both of you need to make this shift.

To begin thinking of your mate as an ally, consider these two things: (1) why you need him and (2) what goals you're invested in together.

Why *Do* You Need Him?

In the 1980s, being deeply attached and in any way dependent on another person came to be seen as unhealthy. But needing someone isn't unhealthy in and of itself. It's only when we become enmeshed—overly needy and easily hooked into destructive patterns—that we damage our relationships.

A friend of mine in her midthirties who recently married told me over coffee how incredibly happy she was. Almost immediately she qualified this, dropping her voice to a confidential whisper, "I've always thought of myself as a feminist, and now here I am deliriously happy because I've found a man to love and depend on. Am I selling out?" Not at all. Being able to really depend on another person is part of what makes a relationship strong and lasting. Interdependency over time is a good and necessary goal.

Can you identify what your mate provides that you need? Include everything: emotional support, sex, financial stability, hugs, his sense of humor, his parenting skills, and anything else that comes to mind. How does he enhance your life? Make it more interesting, secure, or fun? Another way to get in touch with how you need him is by imagining what your life would be like without him. What would you miss the most?

In addition to meeting our tangible needs, our mates should ideally be our spiritual partners. A spiritual partnership is based on the belief that we are together for an important reason. Spiritual partners see themselves as most trusted companions on a long and challenging journey. They are devoted to helping each other grow, achieve their potential, and fulfill their purpose on earth.

What Are Your Shared Goals?

What commitments matter to both of you? Where do your dreams intersect?

"Our children," one woman answers. "Having meaningful and lucrative careers," says another. "Saving the environment" and "Being part of a community," say other women, describing the values and goals they and their mates share.

We are more likely to be allies when our priorities mesh. "I can get really aggravated at Jeff," Pam says, "but then I remember when my mother was dying and he would sit with her in the nursing home for hours, holding her hand. Next to that, the other stuff just doesn't seem that important. My memories of his incredible gentleness make me feel as if we're really together for keeps."

How can you find out your shared goals? Make two columns on a piece of paper. Label one column *Concrete Objectives* and the other *Common Dreams*. A concrete objective might be, "We are saving to move into a house where the children can each have their own room." A common dream expressing more intangible values might be, "We both want to make a difference in the world." The operative word is *both*. Notice where your goals are compatible, and whether you are putting joint energy into meeting them.

PERSONAL CHECKPOINT

- When and in what situations do you turn to your mate?
- Do you feel that you are together for a reason?
- If so, what is that reason?

MUTUAL RESPECT

Being allies not only means reinforcing shared goals. It also means acknowleging and embracing the differences between you.

It bothers us when our partners' values or responses are qualitatively different from our own. We try to tell him about the fight we just had with our best friend, and he says, "I don't see what the big deal is." We iron our daughter's best dress for her spring concert, and he lets her slip out the door in an old sweatshirt and jeans. We make elaborate dinner plans with friends for our anniversary, then find out he'd rather stay home.

Why do these situations infuriate us? Because we equate love with conformity.

"When I was fourteen, I fell in love for the first time," recalls Barb, "I knew it was the real thing because Tim and I had so much in common. He collected comic books; so did I. We both hated the Beatles and adored the Rolling Stones. We only drank root beer, and we were crazy about skiing. We even dressed alike in black turtleneck sweaters, like twins."

Although we eventually grow out of adolescence, we may not grow out of searching for our "twin." We still want our partner to mirror our likes and dislikes. We want him to affirm our reality because that makes us feel safe and understood. It lessens our loneliness, which, according to M. Scott Peck, is the drive behind what we usually call "falling in love." But wanting our partners to be just like us is an immature and ultimately unsatisfying expression of love. Writes Peck:

> The essence of the phenomenon of falling in love is a sudden collapse of an individual's ego boundaries, permitting one to merge his or her identity with that of another person. But sooner or later, in response to the problems of daily living, individual will reasserts itself. He wants to have sex; she doesn't. She wants to go to the movies; he doesn't. He wants to put money in the bank; she wants a dishwasher. . . . One by one, the ego boundaries snap back into place. . . . Once again they are two separate individuals. At this point they begin either to dissolve the ties of their relationship or to initiate the work of real loving.[2]

It's easier to get along with someone who's like us than someone whose opinions, values, or ways of looking at the world threaten or confuse us. It takes real effort to understand another distinctly unique human being, but that's what love requires. Mutual respect means loving another human being— *not in spite of* who they are, but *because of* who they are.

MEN AND WOMEN—OIL AND WATER?

Men and women *are* different. The more I see, the more convinced I am that it's true. Those differences are evident in the ways we process information and relate to other people. The same movie that makes him laugh makes us weep. We want to talk about it and he'd rather not. We're extremely concerned with his approval; he does what he wants without seeming to care much what we think.

"I care a lot about making Martha happy, but half the time I feel as if she were talking in some foreign language," says Frank, a carpenter. "She says she wants intimacy, but I don't know what she means. I've been working since I was nine. I grew up with six brothers, two sisters, three moms, ten thousand baby-sitters, and a dad who was gone all the time. Everybody worked hard. My brothers helped me out of trouble more than once, but we didn't go around touching each other all the time and saying 'I love you.' "

Although many contemporary parents consciously attempt to raise children in a nonsexist fashion, most of us were brought up with an emphasis on gender differences. Dick played with toy horses. Jane played with dolls. Real men were rugged and tough. Real women were tender and compliant. When we become frustrated with our partners because they don't understand us, or our realities clash, it may *not* be that we're personally incompatible, but simply that we've been conditioned to be and act differently.

"I'm my father's son," says Charles, senior vice president of a large corporation. "He was a silent man. I never saw him cry, not even when my brother committed suicide. I'm learning how to cry. I'm learning how to be a better partner. I'm learning to be more sensitive, which is what my wife says she wants. But then when I try to talk to her about my feelings, she seems put off, as if she thought I were a wimp.

"It just seems like everything is on women's terms: what *women* want, what *women* need. Men need to start setting our own boundaries. We need to stop reacting to women and give them strong messages of what *we* want. Men have been shortchanged, too. We're spiritually bereft. We've learned to put on the outer garb of strength, but we haven't developed strength of character."

Charles considers himself to be part of the "men's movement." He is committed to "reaching out for a new definition of manhood—not in reaction to feminism, but to celebrate men's uniqueness."

Whether the source is nature or nurture, the very real differences between the sexes must be acknowledged. Dr. Harville Hendrix points to neuropsychology in exploring the ways men and women experience the world. He says, "Preliminary studies point to the fact that women are easily flooded by emotion and sensation, which is controlled by the right brain, whereas men are more logical and linear, which is the left brain's dominion."[3]

An experience in my own life drove Dr. Hendrix's point home. It was the last night my family would spend in the house we'd lived in for eight years. The walls were bare, the house was scrubbed clean for the new owners, and boxes were piled in every corner.

For the very last time, I tucked the children into their beds in the tiny alcove room they shared. The house was still. I walked from room to room, flooded with memories: bringing Zoe home from the hospital and feeding her in the middle of the night in the rocking chair by the stairs, her tiny finger curled around my ear. Standing in the kitchen talking to my agent on the phone, asking him to repeat very slowly: "Yes. The book is sold." Gary and I curled up on the couch in the den, planning our first seder. Watching my friend Bonnie fall in love with Eugene over Shabbos dinner. The time a bird flew inside and Evan and I camped out on the front yard for three-and-a-half hours, waiting for the firemen who never came.

I picked up my notebook and started to write, images and feelings flowing together as I marked this passage. Tears streaming down my face, I went to find my husband. I sat facing him on the couch in the living room and read to him from my notebook. When I finished, I looked up, waiting for him to say something. He responded casually, "Gee, I guess you'll miss the house."

My mind raced as I registered the extent of what seemed like our estrangement. Clearly Gary couldn't even *begin* to understand who I was or what this meant to me. . . .

But then something amazing happened. My left brain suddenly reached around the back of my head, knocked politely on the door to my right brain, and said: "Excuse me, can we talk?" "Talk about what?" my right brain snorted suspiciously. "Get some information," advised my left brain.

Intrigued, I followed instructions. At the height of my panic, I stopped myself and asked Gary a question: "How do *you* feel about moving?"

"I can't wait," he answered.

A revealing conversation followed. I talked about why I was deeply attached to this house. The house was filled with meaningful turning points. As much as I was looking forward to our new, larger home, I would miss this one a lot.

Gary's associations with the house couldn't have been more different. For eight years his days had begun with getting small, screaming children fed and off to nursery school. After working hard all day, he'd return home to chaos: kids needing attention, dinner to cook, bills, my work taking over the kitchen table. The only time he'd had the house to himself was when he cleaned it, an increasingly impossible task as we outgrew the space. There was clutter everywhere, and he'd walk from room to room like a refugee, with piles of stuff in his arms and nowhere to land. As the coup de grace, he'd spent the past six months restoring the house—cleaning out the basement (an awesome task), replacing door frames, and bleaching hard-water rust stains out of the bathtub and toilets.

No wonder I was so emotional about moving. No wonder he couldn't wait! As we talked, I realized that although we'd lived together under the same roof, we might as well have been in two different worlds. Suddenly I understood that his experience was *his* experience. It was decidedly different from mine, but it in no way invalidated how I felt. Instead of resenting him, I started to care about what he'd been through.

PERSONAL CHECKPOINT

* Name three ways in which you and your partner react very differently in the same situation.
* Which of these differences bother or threaten you?
* Which, if any, of these differences originally attracted you to your mate?

APPRECIATION

When was the last time you complimented your partner or said something nice about your relationship? In describing your marriage, is the first word that pops into your head a negative? When you ask your mate for help, do you steel yourself for him to say no? Deep down, are you afraid to expect too much?

Women who feel shortchanged typically focus on what's missing, instead of being grateful for what we have. The cup is half-empty instead of half-full. For this reason, *appreciation for what is good and strong between us is the final element in the shift from adversaries to allies.*

I admit it; I've always liked the story of Pollyanna. It's sugary, simplistic, and I suppose, naive, but nonetheless I am gripped by the battle between good and evil. I love the fact that a little girl's belief in the world as a good place—a belief facilitated by adversity (falling off a roof and breaking both legs) as well as inspiration (watching the sun's light dance through a shimmer-ing prism)—has the power to transform a town of cynical char-acters into a group of people falling all over themselves trying to be nice to one another.

Being "Pollyannaish" is usually considered an insult, a way of saying, "Open your eyes and quit pretending that problems don't exist!" But women who feel shortchanged don't need en-couragement to list our grievances. We're well aware of the problems in our relationships, so much so that we forget to count our blessings and appreciate what we have.

Counting our blessings is a way of consciously bringing more abundance into our relationships. Two techniques are useful: *taking stock* of what's satisfying, and measuring our relationships in terms of *growth* rather than *perfection*.

Taking Stock

Often we think that happiness is one thing when it's really another. We may think our happiness depends on our mates living up to a certain image, having the right career, or making enough money. We're surprised to discover that what we *think* we want doesn't always translate into what makes us happy.

"I always envisioned myself with an artist," says Joanne, a self-described sixties flower child who, at forty-one, has turned her artistic talent into a thriving tie-dye business. "I was a hippie. I dated guys with long hair, who smoked pot and listened to the Grateful Dead. Guys who were creative."

When Joanne met Rick at an apparel market, she was imme-diately attracted, even though he wasn't her usual type. A sales representative for a women's ready-to-wear line, Rick was the consummate businessman, Brooks Brothers all the way. "We're opposites," Joanne laughs. "He likes steak; I like sushi. He plays racquetball; I play chess. When my friends met him they thought I had flipped. They couldn't see us together and neither could I. . . . You know, when you imagine the two of you together in a photograph on the mantle . . . I couldn't make it fit."

STRATEGY FOR BUILDING MUTUAL RESPECT

Tell yourself "I am who I am and my mate is who he is. We are separate individuals with equally important gifts to bring to our relationship."

Don't tell him "I'll never understand you."

Do tell him "I'd like to understand the way you think about or do _____. Could you please try to explain it to me?"

The risk He'll think you're criticizing or patronizing him.

The reward A enhanced appreciation of each other.

Despite her reservations (and her friends' blatant disapproval), Joanne married Rick. Two years into their marriage, she says, "There are still times when I look at Rick and wonder how I ever could have married him. Just the other day, I started a philosophical discussion with him and he said, 'Get to the point,' as if you could just sum it up in thirty seconds.

"On the other hand, he helps me not to take myself so seriously. I'm moody, and he's matter-of-fact. We balance each other. And I've come to respect how successful he is in business. In its own way, business is an art.

"But mostly, he makes me really happy. And it's funny: Now, when I see pictures of us together, we look just right."

It's important to discern between old, dusty ideas of what

we've always thought would make us happy—the "perfect guy" ideal we've been polishing since age thirteen—and what is truly fulfilling to us as adult women. Counting our blessings means giving up preconceived notions, other peoples' judgments, old images, and romantic illusions, all of which blind us to our true feelings. It means thinking of ourselves as happy, in at least some parts of our relationships, and spelling them out.

WHAT DO YOU LIKE ABOUT HIM?

To do this exercise, simply list ten things you like (better yet, love) about your mate. If you can come up with ten, make it twenty-five. If you hit twenty-five, go for fifty.

Be as specific as possible; you'll think of more that way. And don't qualify any good feelings. If you write down, "He notices when I cut my hair," don't add, "except last Friday when he didn't say a word." If you include, "He makes great lasagna," but then you remember that he hasn't taken a turn washing dishes in two weeks, keep writing. Negatives don't cancel out the positives; the goal is to get in touch with all the wonderful reasons to keep healing and improving your relationship.

This is one list well worth saving. Post it where you can look at it whenever you're feeling discouraged. Or share it with your mate; being privy to what you like about him is great positive reinforcement.

Growth Versus Perfection

The Perfection Scale, which we typically apply to relationships, is based on impossible, unreachable standards. When perfection is the goal, our mate can't possibly begin to measure up. We are continually disappointed because we're focused on how he hasn't made it all the way.

The Growth Scale, on the other hand, emphasizes improvement rather than perfection.[4] Instead of judging our mates' behavior on a scale of one to ten, where ten is the only acceptable reading, we are more interested in incremental movement upward. Any growth in the right direction—even if it's only from one to two, two to three, and then three to four—is considered a positive sign.

The following diagram illustrates the difference between the Growth Scale and the Perfection Scale:

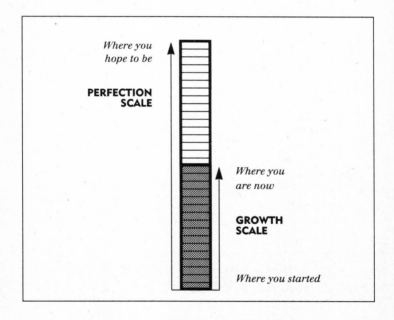

Measuring relationships on a Growth Scale makes our appreciation soar because the emphasis is on success rather than failure. The question to ask is "How far has he come?" not "Is he all the way there yet?" As long as he's trying, as long as you can see progress, there's every reason to reinvest.

HE MAY NEVER BE YOUR BEST FRIEND

An ally isn't necessarily a friend. Giving up being adversarial doesn't mean that you always like him or never blame him, or even that you always get along. Some couples are close friends. Some don't talk much, but can't keep their hands off each other. Other, perfectly suited pairs thrive on passion and conflict. It's their style. June and Ward were friends; Taylor and Burton weren't. But that didn't keep them from being the loves of each other's lives.

For some, friendship comes with time. For some, marriage is always stormy. Anna Quindlen wrote this about her own marriage: "Our relationship is too judgmental, too demanding, too prickly to have much in common with the quiet waters of friendship. Like emotional acupuncturists, we know just where to put the needle. And do. But we are each others' family."[5] Finally, being allies is about being family in the very best sense of the word.

SPIRITUALITY: SUSTAINING APPRECIATION

Appreciation isn't something we suddenly decide to have and *boom*, we're overflowing with it. It takes time—some say a lifetime—to stop feeling shortchanged and start feeling grateful for what we have.

It is with fits and starts that we make such a profound shift. Something happens that makes us aware of our gratefulness: Last night was romantic, the kids are finally back to school after three miserable days of the flu, and the proposal is not only finished but it looks like a winner. We feel expansive and hopeful; the world looks like a pretty nice place.

Then, Casanova calls and says he's had a sudden business dinner come up. There's an urgent message from the school nurse on the answering machine. The proposal is rejected, and to add insult to injury, that loose crown falls out in a toasted English muffin. Once again, the world seems shaky and sinister.

How do we sustain an attitude of appreciation? Ultimately, appreciation is based in spirituality, in a deep sense of security that we are supported by the universe. Knowing we are supported increases our feelings of independence. We can choose to be in a relationship or not, knowing that if we had to, we could survive alone. Being in an intimate relationship begins to seem more like a wonderful addition to our lives than something we can't possibly live without.

When we feel spiritually connected, we are less buffeted by external events. We are directed by an inner sense of purpose that helps us hold firm to our commitment. And spirituality nurtures a deep sense of awe and gratitude that enhances our appreciation of our mate. We become acutely aware that he, just like us, is a human being doing his best to navigate his life, and that it is indeed a privilege to share the journey.

You know you're in the process of making the shift from adversaries to allies *when you feel ready to start depending on your mate as your true partner in life.*

AFTERWORD

We have stopped shortchanging ourselves when we complete the shift from ambivalence to commitment, from anger to empowerment, and from adversaries to allies.

Now we are ready to make an informed decision. We are ready to say "I will be fully in this relationship" or "I have done everything possible to make this a better relationship, but it is time to say good-bye."

Neither is simple. Either choice requires loving our mates—and loving ourselves.

None of us is really prepared for the immense task of loving another human being. We are handicapped going into it. We expect our partners to perform impossible feats in the name of love. We want them to make us safe and happy and fulfilled, and no wonder we are disillusioned. We expect love to be simple, when in fact it's the hardest challenge in life.

The difficulty lies in the paradoxes. We try to pin love down like a butterfly under a glass, but it defies such staid definition. We need to turn it up and down and around in our hands, looking at all sides of the questions that make love both an intensely real feeling and the greatest mystery on earth.

Loving another person requires that we approach our partners with a willingness to grapple with these paradoxes:

- Love means subduing one's ego.
- Love means asserting one's power.

- Love requires absolute trust and intimacy.
- Love requires total independence.

- Love asks that we transcend our expectations.
- Love asks that we expect miracles.

- Love rests on making a commitment in the present.
- Love rests on the ability to withstand change.

- Love depends on infinite tolerance.
- Love depends on respectful confrontation.
-
  Love is fleeting.
- Love is forever.

Women who stop feeling shortchanged are less concerned with being right for the sake of being right. At the same time, we are confident in saying what we want and defending our take on reality.

Women who stop feeling shortchanged are vulnerable and willing to bend. Yet we know that intimacy requires a strong and deep sense of self.

Women who stop being shortchanged adjust expectations to meet reality, freeing us to welcome all the possibilities.

Women who stop being shortchanged commit to being all the way "in" our relationships. We're ready to start *right now*— but we expect change and are flexible when it comes.

Women who stop being shortchanged understand that much of what we call "love"—especially romance—ebbs and flows. But we are secure in the knowledge that real love, when nurtured, creates lasting, intimate partnerships.

Loving—A New Perspective

Even when we accept the paradoxes of love, we may not stop feeling shortchanged. What trips us up when we are clearly so interested in finding love? The answer is that we are looking for the wrong thing. We don't understand that love is not the destination. Loving is.

We become disillusioned when we focus on the ways we don't get the love we want and need. Surely it is important to be honest with ourselves if we've discovered that our partner doesn't fulfill our most fundamental needs. But anyone who has ever truly been happy with another person knows that loving is infinitely more satisfying than being loved.

Hillary, who left her husband of two years and has recently remarried, experienced this firsthand. "Everyone thought I divorced Drew because he couldn't satisfy me," she says, "but they were wrong. I left when I realized that no matter how hard I tried, no matter how much professional help we got, I would never be able to love Drew the way I knew I could love someone. That was so painful, but I knew it was true and I knew what I had to do.

"This marriage is a different story," she says. "I'm really in love with Isaac. The way I know is that I get so much pleasure from giving to him. Loving him makes me feel good. It brings out the best in me."

When we are loving, we like ourselves better. And there's a much better chance that our intimate relationships will improve. It's rare for one partner to stop blaming and start being more supportive, cooperative, and loving without its profoundly affecting the quality of a relationship. However, expect change to take time. Making the shifts suggested here is a long-term proposition. It will take considerable time to determine if and how your relationship has changed or is changing for the better.

Ultimately, whether it is or isn't matters less than how we, as individuals, change and grow. If we are truly able to make a commitment to our mates, we will have deepened our own strength of character. We will be more able to stand behind commitments in our work, with our children, in friendships, and in our communities. If we are truly empowered, we won't allow ourselves to be victims anywhere, under any circumstances. We will insist on being heard, and being treated with respect. If we have been allies, we will be able to stay or leave in peace, knowing that we have given our all.

Having finished my own journey to stop being short-changed, I sadly discovered that in my case, loving Gary—and myself—made it necessary to leave him. Although our marriage markedly improved, having done everything possible to improve communications, to heal the past, and to reinvest fully, I came to know, in the bottom of my heart, that we were not meant to be life partners. I had always believed that if I just tried hard enough, I could make it work. But insurmountable differences made it impossible. Ending our marriage was a decision marked by enormous pain, but one I made in peace.

Intimate relationships are a microcosm of who we are and how we conduct ourselves in all other spheres of life. They are a wonderful place to practice patience and tolerance. They provide the opportunity to develop character; to learn how to trust others and set boundaries that let love in, without losing ourselves. They are a place to heal and to try out new, healthier behavior, and to get more in touch with feelings of gratitude and awe.

If, in order to stop being shortchanged, you must bid farewell to a loved one, then take these lessons with you wherever you may go. If it is right to take a few cautious steps forward with your mate, then know that this is a great beginning. If you are ready to reinvest fully, apply what you have learned to the task of transforming your relationship—then begin the journey. Go with confidence and with grace.

Chapter Notes

Chapter One: Shortchanged

1. Martha Weinman Lear, "The New Marital Therapy," *The New York Times Magazine*, March 6, 1988.

2. Betty Friedan, *The Second Stage*, Summit Books, New York, 1981.

3. Anna Quindlen, *Living Out Loud*, Random House, New York, 1988.

4. "How to Stay Married," *Newsweek*, August 24, 1987.

5. Reported by Eloise Salholz, "The Marriage Crunch," *Newsweek*, June 2, 1986. The authors of the research paper, "Marriage Patterns in the United States," are Neil G. Bennett, Patricia H. Craig, and David E. Bloom.

6. Cynthia Smith, *Why Women Shouldn't Marry*, Lyle Stuart, Secaucus, N.J., 1988.

Chapter Two: Putting Up the Wall

1. Merle Shain, *Some Men Are More Perfect Than Others*, J. B. Lippincott, Philadelphia, 1973.

Chapter Three: Babies, Bills, and Better Things to Do

1. Barbara J. Berg, *The Crisis of the Working Mother*, Summit Books, New York, 1986.

2. 1990 *Yankelovich Monitor,* reprinted in the *Minneapolis-St. Paul Star Tribune,* March 10, 1991.

3. Marian Burros, "Women: Out of the House but Not Out of the Kitchen," *Homemaking,* February 2, 1988, courtesy of Catalyst, Inc., New York.

4. Arlie Hochschild, *The Second Shift,* Penguin Books, New York, 1989.

5. *The Kinsey Institute New Report on Sex; What You Need to Be Sexually Literate,* 1990.

6. Janet Reynold, "DINS dilemma: Double Income, No Sex," *Hartford* (Connecticut) *Advocate* reprinted in the *Utne Reader,* September/October 1988.

7. Katherine Barrett, "Why Don't We Talk Anymore?" *Ladies Home Journal,* September 1986.

CHAPTER FOUR: I WANT A MAN WHO CAN DANCE!

1. Stephanie Covington, *Leaving the Enchanted Forest,* Harper & Row, New York, 1988.

2. Albert Ellis, *A New Guide to Rational Living,* Institute for Rational Living/Prentice-Hall Press, New York, 1975.

CHAPTER FIVE: BURIED TREASURE

1. Harville Hendrix, *Getting the Love You Want,* Harper & Row, New York, 1989.

2. Melody Beattie, *Beyond Codependency And Getting Better All The Time,* Harper & Row, New York, 1989.

3. Susan Forward, *Toxic Parents,* Bantam Books, New York, 1989.

4. Gershen Kaufman, *Shame: The Power of Caring;* Schenkman, Rochester, V.T., 1985.

5. Harriet Goldhor Lerner, *The Dance of Intimacy,* Harper & Row, New York, 1989.

CHAPTER SIX: UNDERCURRENTS AND TIDAL WAVES

1. The concept of guilt vs. guilty fear was first brought to my attention by Minneapolis therapist Dr. William Goodman.

2. Carol Botwin, *Men Who Can't Be Faithful,* Copestone Press/Warner Books, New York, 1988.

CHAPTER NINE: FROM SELF-VICTIMIZATION TO EMPOWERMENT

1. The idea of positive intentions was shared with me by Dr. Charlotte Davis Kasl, who referenced the work of Ken Keyes, *Handbook to Higher Consciousness,* Love Line Books, 1989.

CHAPTER TEN: FROM ADVERSARIES TO ALLIES

1. Alfie Kohn, *No Contest: The Case against Competition,* Houghton Mifflin Co., Boston, 1986.

2. M. Scott Peck, *The Road Less Traveled,* Simon & Schuster, New York, 1980.

3. Harville Hendrix, *Getting the Love You Want,* Harper & Row, New York, 1989.

4. Many thanks to Jill Marks, whose insight into perfection and growth prompted me to create this scale.

5. Anna Quindlen, *Living Out Loud,* Random House, New York, 1988.

ABOUT THE AUTHOR

ELLEN SUE STERN
nationally known speaker, founder of
Expecting Change workshops, and faculty
member of the Institute of Integral
Development, has helped thousands of
women and men in their recovery from
indispensability. Her work has appeared
in such national magazines as *New
Woman, Self, Parenting,* and *Woman's
Day.* She lives in Minneapolis.